KYRGIOS

THE SMASH HITS
Nick vs The World

Sam Harvey and Harv

WITH CHRIS MCLEOD

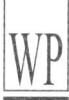

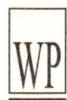

Published by:
Wilkinson Publishing Pty Ltd
ACN 006 042 173
Level 6, 174 Collins St, Melbourne, Victoria, Australia 3000
Ph: +61 3 9654 5446
enquiries@wilkinsonpublishing.com.au

 WilkinsonPublishing
 wilkinsonpublishinghouse
 WPBooks

A catalogue record of this book is available from the
National Library of Australia.
ISBN(s): 9781922810274

All Illustrations © by Paul Harvey.

Transcripts from by ASAP Sports.
Statistics from WTA Press Center.

Design: Michael Bannenberg.
Printed and bound in Australia by Ligare Book Printers.

CONTENTS

INTRODUCTION

Nick Kyrgios is a complex character. He has undoubted talent as a tennis player, possibly even a Grand Slam singles trophy to match the doubles victory achieved with Thanasi Kokkinakis in the 2022 Australian Open. But there's another side to him, a dark side that doesn't endear himself to traditionalists and has some referring to him as a ticking timebomb.

Few other players display the level of emotion that he has done throughout his career.

He played his first match on the ATP Tour in 2013. Nine years later he was enjoying his best season ever, winning titles and defeating top 10 players including the World No.1.

He became a Wimbledon finalist but he's also one of the most penalised players in world professional tennis.

Anyone with even just a passing interest in tennis will have a view about him, whether it is a former Wimbledon champion such as John McEnroe or Pat Cash, or an eight-year-old starting out in a Hot Shots program. Some will detest him; others will be fans.

His name isn't usually mentioned in the same breath as Australia's most recent tennis champion, Ash Barty, who won three women's Grand Slams – the French, the Australian and The Open at Wimbledon – before retiring gracefully and with accolades aplenty.

The Kyrgios way isn't the Barty way and it is doubtful that when he puts his racquets away for good he will be remembered with the same reverence as Ash Barty.

He was 27 years old when he reached the final at Wimbledon in 2022 and should have had a few good years of tennis left, if injuries don't intervene and he still has the will to win. That's a big "if" of course.

He was troubled by knee soreness twice during the US swing and even hinted that the end of his career might not be far away, although few took that seriously.

So, why does he play tennis? He has said he doesn't like the game much. In a 2016 interview he said: "I definitely don't love the sport... there is zero chance that Nick Kyrgios will be playing tennis when he's 30 years old."

His motivation has often been questioned. He's even been accused of tanking – losing a set deliberately. Sometimes he is highly motivated, sometimes he isn't. Motivation comes and goes.

"I'm just trying to not let people down," Kyrgios said after beating Daniil Medvedev for the second time in 2022. "I was in this press conference room a while back and I lost in the third round, it was the worst feeling because I've just got so much expectation. I'm finally able to show it now. I feel like I've been working really hard. I've just got a lot of motivation at the moment."

Kyrgios is good at tennis. At least he is when he puts his mind and body to it. Perhaps wanting to win a "major", one of four Grand Slams played worldwide, is enough motivation to keep him going after all.

He got close in 2022, aged 27, and if a Slam is his aim and

by his reckoning, he'd have three years left to achieve one. After reaching the Wimbledon final in 2022 it seemed he found a new interest in Grand Slams, setting himself for the US Open just over a month later and posting his best results there by reaching the quarter-finals.

Previously, he'd played down his interest in Grand Slams: "I don't have a doubt that if I wanted to win Grand Slams, I would commit. I'd train two times a day. I'd go to the gym every day. I'd stretch. I'd rehab. I'd eat right."

But by August 2022 just weeks ahead of the US Open he was focussed on getting a seeding so he could avoid the top 10 players at least until later rounds.

And after losing the quarter-final at the US Open in September 2022, for the first time he conceded winning Grand Slams is now the only thing that will satisfy him.

He has rarely talked about what he earns, but according to those who record such figures, he has done nicely – more than $A 18 million on the ATP Tour in the nine years since he turned professional (plus endorsements as well).

He likes to beat the world's best. Over his career he has claimed some prized scalps – Nadal, Federer, Djokovic – all No. 1 players. In the US in 2022, he took down the World No. 1 Daniil Medvedev twice in the space of 30 days, costing the Russian his top ranking.

He's always confident when he takes on anyone ranked higher than him: "I feel like I'm one of the best players in the world tactically," he once said. And: "It's better to be the underdog than have all the pressure, for sure." But he also once said: "I think when things get tough, I'm just a little bit soft."

Attitudes to Kyrgios are tempered by what people see on the world's tennis courts. Now that Kyrgios is a Wimbledon finalist, the pinnacle of his then nine-year career, more people have seen the many sides of him. He's the player with a touch of genius but also the player who can be defaulted during a match for throwing a tantrum.

He is his own man.

Nike became one of his sponsors from an early time. He went on to the court against friend Thanasi Kokkinakis in the 2015 Australian Open boys final in 2913 wearing a "lucky" shirt that was 18 months old. It wasn't Nike's latest and they weren't impressed.

Another time he wanted to play in a singlet so he cut the sleeves off his shirt. He's complained about blinking lights, people talking, people smoking, lack of support from his player's box ... it's a long list.

To many coaches and players, he doesn't play by the old rules – "This is how the game is", "this is how the game should be played."

That's not the Kyrgios way. So, where has his way taken him?

A Wimbledon final of course.

He reached a career-high ranking of No. 13 in 2019. He would have returned to the Top 30 had rankings points been on offer at Wimbledon (they weren't because players from Russia and Belarus were banned in response to the Russian assault on Ukraine). Reaching the quarter-finals at Flushing Meadows moved him back into the Top 20 at 18, for the time being at least and Australians No. 1 men's player.

Kyrgios has critics, many. He also has a fan club, started during the Australian Open in 2022.

Just what makes Kyrgios tick isn't clear, perhaps not even to himself.

He has been relatively forthcoming about his progress through the ranks to become a Wimbledon finalist, beaten in 2022 in four sets (4-6, 6-3, 6-4, 7-6) by a legend of the game, Novak Djokovic, himself a controversial figure but in a different way.

In Kyrgios's own words after his quarterfinal win: "There was a time where I was having to be forced out of a pub at 4 a.m. to play Nadal second round (2019). My agent had to come get me out of a pub at 4 a.m. before I played my match on Centre Court Wimbledon. I've come a long way, that's for sure."

How well do we really know him? At a post-match press conference, he was asked about how he saw himself compared to other players. His response: "Well, none of you really know me at all. Like, you don't hang out with me at all. You only kind of see what you see on the court. It's always been a bit of a roller coaster. So I understand how it's mixed reviews."

Does he care how he is perceived? "I just feel like I'm comfortable in my own skin," is his answer. Fair call.

He has had some dark moments – self harm, booze and drugs

were part of that darkness, and he isn't reluctant to talk about them. He has had self-doubts, but Wimbledon in 2022 seemed to give him new confidence. His achievements in the US Open after that reinforced his ability and renewed self-belief.

He explained after the Wimbledon final: "There was a point where I was almost done with the sport... I posted (on Instagram) this year about the kind of mental state I was in in 2019 when I was at the Australian Open with self-harm and suicidal thoughts and stuff. I'm sitting there today after the match... to be a semi-finalist at Wimbledon, it's a special accomplishment for everyone, but I think especially for me.

"I don't think anyone would have – if you asked anyone if I was able to do that the last couple years, I think everyone would have probably said: No, he doesn't have the mental capacity, he doesn't have the fitness capacity, he doesn't have the discipline, all that. I almost started doubting myself with all that traffic coming in and out of my mind.

"I just sat there today and soaked it all in. There's just so many people I want to thank. At the same time I feel like I don't want to stop here either."

And he didn't – going all the way to the last 8 at the US Open, yet bitterly disappointed he didn't go further.

"I feel like these four tournaments are the only ones that are ever gonna matter, and it's like you have to start it all again, and I have to wait until Australian Open," he said.

"It's devastating. It's heartbreaking. Not just for me, it's for everyone I know that wants me to win."

Complex, but an undoubted talent with racquet in hand. We can expect to see more of him.

This book delves into the career of a young slightly obese Canberra boy who rose to become one of the most controversial and divisive players of modern tennis – and a Wimbledon finalist. Just what does make him tick?

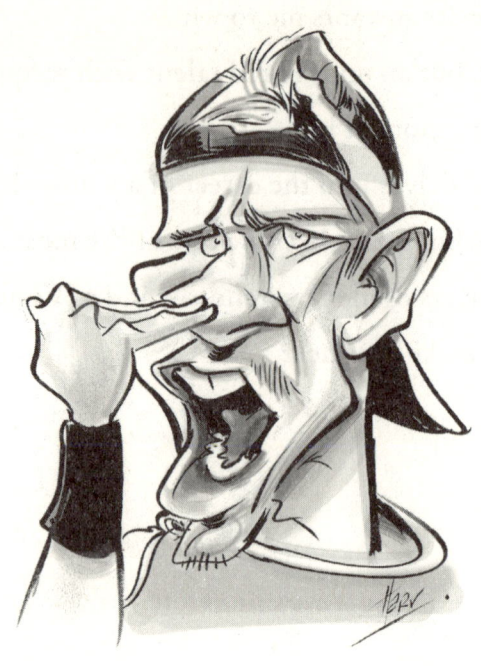

"The only great that's ever been supportive of me the whole time has been Lleyton Hewitt...
He kind of knows that I kind of do my own thing. I'm definitely the outcast of the Australian players. It sucks."

NICK KYGRIOS

POT, KETTLE!

Tennis was created as a wholesome game by monks in 12th Century France as a respite from prayer and a welcome distraction from fasting and celibacy.

It was soon adopted in and around the 1800s by English, Spanish, German, and Dutch aristocrats who saw the game as a gentile pastime, played by the most sophisticated and polished of their kind.

They may have wished it remained an elegant, "gentleman's game" forever played by paragons like Rod Laver and Fred Stolle, then Pat Rafter and Ash Barty.

Sadly, tennis has seen many fall below the behavioural standard of the demi-gods. For every Federer there's a Gonzales. For every Barty there's a Capriati. The tennis rogue's gallery is long and perturbing with the shining crowns of some of its greatest tarnished and dented. None of this is surprising.

Are tennis players not human? To err is in their nature. What is surprising, however, is how short is the memory of many flawed champions when asked to voice or write their opinions of Nick Kyrgios.

Kyrgios is pigeonholed as the Bad Boy of Tennis; maddingly, it's the boys and girls for whom the term was invented that seem to be the most desperate to pass on the mantle.

Australia's 1987 Wimbledon champion Pat Cash launched a scathing tirade on Kyrgios, labelling him a "cheat" and saying on the BBC, "He's brought Tennis to the lowest level I can see as far as gamesmanship, cheating, manipulation, abuse, aggressive behaviour to umpires, to linesmen. Something has got to be done about it. It's just an absolute circus."

This is from a man who once hurled a racket into the stands after a loss to the robotic Ivan Lendl, received a $US 5,000 fine for vile language and racket abuse in Germany in 1987, and in 1997 destroyed a courtside television microphone after a dodgy line-call at Sandton Gardens in a match against Tim Wilkison.

To be fair, Cash has never been one for the carefully considered comment. He famously referred to women's tennis as "two sets of rubbish over in half an hour."

Cash declared in his 2002 autobiography *Uncovered: The Autobiography of Pat Cash* that the pressure of the centre stage saw him smoke marijuana every night during his first crack at Wimbledon. Cash said he found himself suicidal and dependant on cocaine after injuries in 1985 and often attended drug-fuelled parties hosted by Australian Open champion and notorious playboy Vitas Gerulaitis. Intriguingly, he has failed to show support towards Kyrgios, who recently spoke about his own suicidal thoughts and depression.

Nick Kyrgios has decried the lack of support Aussie greats have given him. He has been hurt by it, but he may be pleased to hear he is not on his own. The slamming of the up-and-comer is not new to tennis. John Newcombe once wrote an article comparing Mats Wilander and Pat Cash, saying "The comparison between the abilities of Wilander and Cash makes the Grand Canyon look like a crack in your living room plaster", he also said Cash "didn't possess the qualities of a true champion."

The subtle difference here is Newcombe had an exemplary record, a paragon of the sport who was never anything but gracious as a winner. He showed full respect for opponents, umpires, ball-boys, and lines people alike. Cash was anything but, once breaking the largest fine in Australian Open history record in 1992 ($US 9,000). This was subsequently passed by none other than "Super-Brat" John McEnroe, another sometimes Kyrgios critic, who once accused him of "disrespecting the game!"

John McEnroe was at times a menace on the court, famously disqualified and booted from the Australian Open mid-game in 1990.

Like Kyrgios, McEnroe polarised fans. He was giddily talented, winning seven Grand Slam men's singles titles. This German-born (to US parents) hot-head became synonymous with on-court tantrums.

After tensions with the crowd and players alike in the 1980 Wimbledon qualifying games, McEnroe was booed on to centre court in his final against Bjorn Borg yet won back their admiration with his skill in one of the greatest finals in history, Borg winning 1-6, 7-5, 6-3, 6-7 (16-18), 8-6 in the match the lasted three hours and 53 minutes.

Back at home in the US, McEnroe gained revenge when he defeated Borg in the 1980 US Open. In his next tournament

McEnroe dialled the nastiness up to 11.

Back in London for Wimbledon in 1981, he left no stone unturned in his efforts to fire himself up, kick-starting things in his first-round match against fellow American Tom Gullikson. Serving to Gullikson, McEnroe thought he aced his opponent until chair umpire Ted James called it out. Blowing steam, McEnroe approached James near the net and uttered the famous line, "Chalk came up all over the place. You can't be serious, man."

His follow up roar, "YOU CANNOT BE SERIOUS!" shook the cream from the strawberries and rattled the tennis establishment to the core. Mac followed up with, "Everybody knows it's in – the whole stadium – and you call it out? Explain that to me, will you?"

When it was Gullikson's turn to serve, McEnroe unleashed again, directing his attention towards James and the tournament referee Fred Hoyles, calling them the "absolute pits of the world."

Despite the outburst, McEnroe would advance into the Wimbledon Final against Bjorn Borg, defeating him 4-6, 7-6, 7-6, 6-4. He was fined $US 1,500 for his first-round behaviour and became the first Wimbledon winner in history not to gain automatic membership into the All-England Club.

Would Kyrgios have been selected if he won Wimbledon in 2022? It would take a lot for Kyrgios to top McEnroe's long, long list of infringements. At 30 years of age, McEnroe became the first Tennis player to be disqualified from an event, at the 1990 Australian Open.

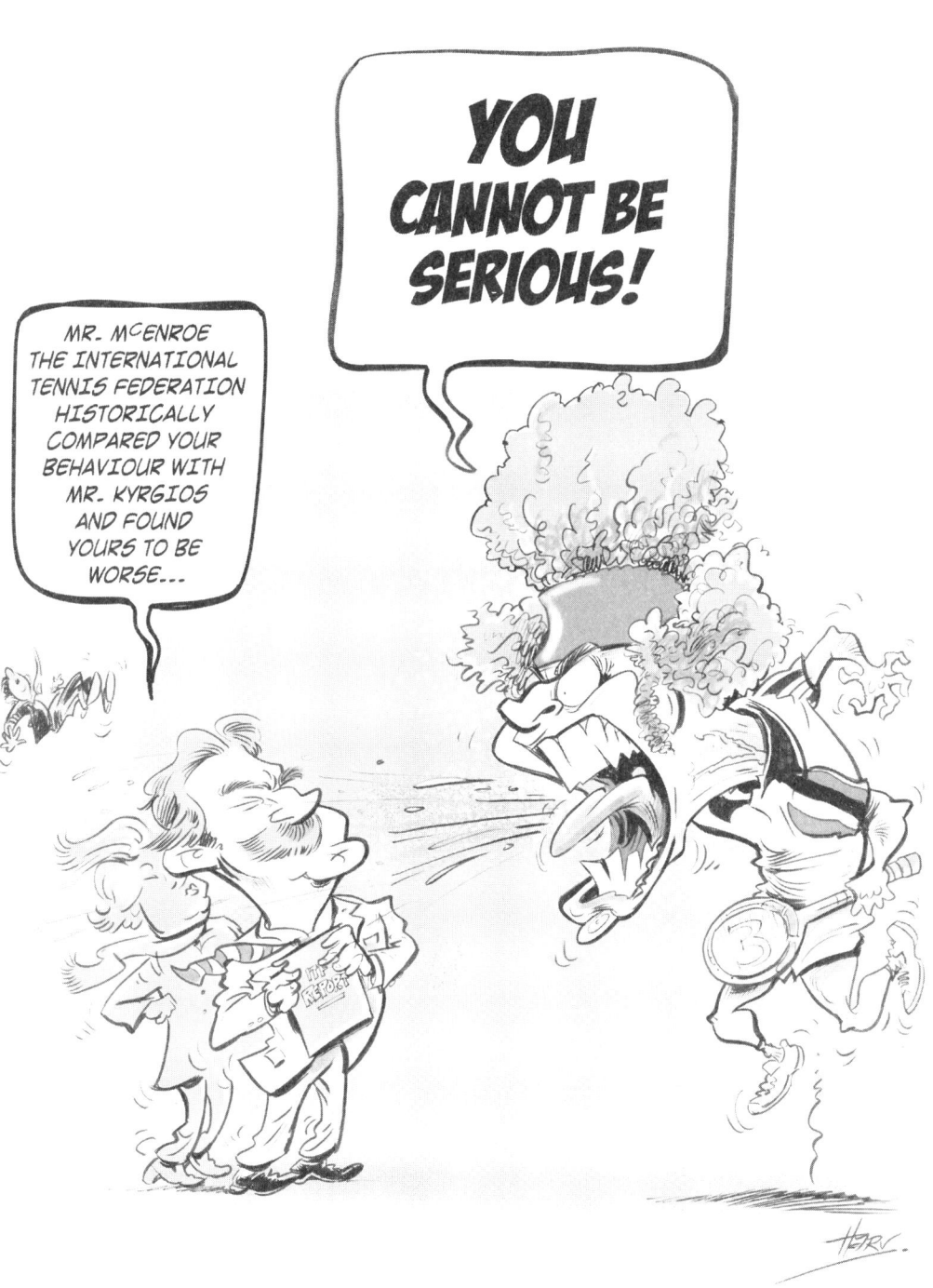

In his fourth-round match against Swedish player Mikael Pernfors, he was given a code violation for staring down the umpire after throwing his racket on the ground and intimidating a line judge. Under instructions from the Australian Open tournament supervisor Ken Farrar, chair umpire Gerry Armstrong defaulted McEnroe for the third code of conduct violation, awarding the match to Pernfors and disqualified McEnroe.

If you watched Kyrgios's Wimbledon final against Djokovic, you would, have seen his "the one who looks like she's had about 700 drinks bro" appeal to chair umpire Renaud Lichtenstein, after he became increasingly agitated with a female in the crowd yelling/talking to him during games and even while he was serving.

The woman was escorted out and eventually allowed to return. She said after the match she had consumed only two drinks and had been encouraging Kyrgios.

Ironically, this incident resembled McEnroe's experience at the 1990 US Open when he argued with a female spectator. McEnroe screamed at the chair umpire, "She's yelling right in the middle of my serve." Furiously McEnroe halted the game, marched over to the spectator, and berated her from the sidelines.

The irony wouldn't be lost on anyone when they read that McEnroe questioned Kyrgios's sanity. McEnroe wrote that Kyrgios was a "genius" who desperately needed a one-on-one session with the father of psychoanalysis, Sigmund Freud.

"He needs Sigmund Freud to come out of the grave and somehow figure out a way to keep this guy going..." Going on to say, "He's obviously tortured in certain ways."

Sadly, McEnroe, who freely admitted to seeing "37 therapists" in his self-titled documentary *McEnroe* released on 15 July 2022 conceded the therapists, cocaine use or his infidelity were unable to cure his anger problems. He wrote the book on boorish tennis behaviour. Some of his views on Kyrgios would seem to be the blackest of a pot calling out the kettle.

A cavalcade of past greats lined up to pot-shot Kyrgios whenever they got the chance.

In various world newspapers and across myriad social media platforms, Kyrgios is described as everything from a "naughty boy" to the "spawn of satan."

His ability is rarely questioned, although his lack of a top ten ranking is often mentioned.

Kyrgios being bad for tennis seems to be a nonsensical argument. If tennis could survive Ilie Nastase, Jimmy Connors, John McEnroe and so many other miscreants, it will survive Nick Kyrgios.

It's true that code violations, foul-mouth tirades, and controversy litter the career of Kyrgios. Yet if we are to compare apples and oranges, the Americans, who are so free with their condemnation of Kyrgios, created new benchmarks for court petulance and questionable gamesmanship and then raised it again and again until it threatened to tear the very fabric of the game asunder.

Andre Agassi admitted in his autobiography published on 9 November 2009, *Open: An Autobiography*, that he snorted crystal methamphetamine in 1997 and lied when he tested positive to escape a ban. Then who could forget Jeff Tarango and his infamous meltdown, which saw him default at Wimbledon in 1995. His wife infamously slapped chair umpire Bruno Rebeuh after the game.

There seems to be a common theme across the tennis landscape that past misdemeanours are forgotten and often forgiven once you've been retired for more than a decade.

Jimmy Connors was the jester. A champion of working-class Americans, yet he so often abused his opponents, the linesmen, and the umpires that his matches were like car crashes – watched through splayed fingers, yet impossible to look away from them.

Although he was one of the more gifted tennis players ever to play the game, tennis remembers Jimmy Connors for his outbursts and tantrums on the court. A sportsman who cared little about what the public thought of him, Connors polarised more fans than Kyrgios has ever done. One section of the crowd (mainly his patriots) loved and idolised his combative, anti-establishment toughness, his never-say-die attitude, and rebellious character. Another section of the crowd marvelled at his tennis, with many modern stars crediting Connors for his raw power and two-handed backhand, instrumental in the modern game.

Connors used his aggression and emotion to build the feeling in the crowd. He regularly riled himself into a frenzy if he noticed the momentum was turning in favour of his opponent.

The American crowds loved his enthusiasm and self-belief,

yet it often crossed the border into the realm of insanity. It didn't matter if the crowd loved or hated him; Connors suckled on the energy, and he exploited the pandemonium towards linesmen, officials, and his opponent.

At his peak, Connors was never far from the headlines. In 1974, he was banned from the French Open by the French Tennis Federation President Philippe Chatrier after signing with a rival professional circuit, the World Team Tennis League, in the US.

Though he missed Roland Garros that year, Connors was victorious at Wimbledon, the Australian Open, and US Open in the same year, just missing the chance to join Rod Laver as the Grand Slam winner in all four Grand Slam singles titles during a calendar year.

Connors then filed a suit in the French courts seeking the right to participate and eventually sued the FTF, seeking $US 200,000 (a massive amount of money back then) for damages. Connors was booed at Wimbledon in 1977 after he snubbed the parade of champions on the first day of the centenary year. He said later he "completely forgot" the event was on.

Fast forward to the US Open in 1991, and tennis fans were treated to an enormous Connors explosion. At 39 years old, Connors was well and truly in the twilight of his career, and his last Slam singles title was eight years before, in the 1983 US Open.

By now No. 174 in the World, Connors was a wild-card entrant and surprised all doubters by moving into the fourth round when he faced No. 10 and compatriot Aaron Krickstein, a

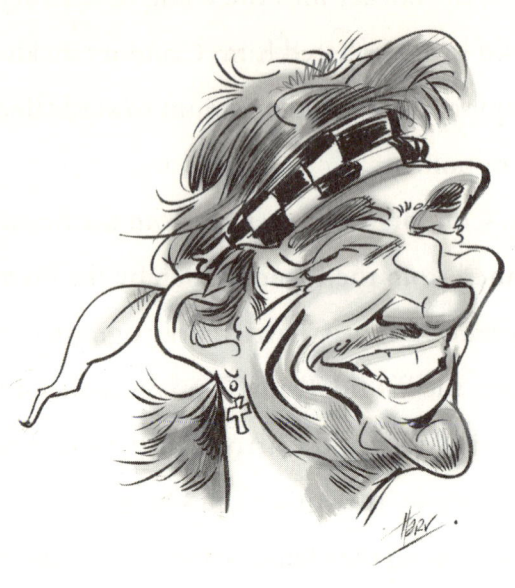

"He's brought Tennis to the lowest level I can see as far as gamesmanship, cheating, manipulation, abuse, aggressive behaviour to umpires, to linesmen. Something has got to be done about it. It's just an absolute circus."

Pat Cash

young up-and-comer who was 15 years his junior.

After losing the first set, Connors used his showmanship and experience to work himself and the crowd into a frenzy. After forcing the second set into a tiebreaker, Connors played at a ball that was called out. He unleashed the mother of all tantrums! Connors let rip at chair umpire David Littlefield, declaring, "I'm out here playing my butt off at 39 years old, and you're doing that... Get your ass out of the chair. You're a bum. You're a bum!"

Littlefield didn't report Connors, despite the ebullient American calling him an "abortion." Connors would go on to win the match in five sets, proving that his antics and on-court bullying often worked in his favour. Though he played a fellow compatriot, the US crowd loved to feed off his rebelliousness and combativeness.

As far as bad boys of tennis go, one name stands head and shoulders above Kyrgios, McEnroe, and Connors. That name is Ilie Nastase. He was nicknamed "Nasty" because it sounds similar to his name and partly because on and off the court Nastase was really not a nice bloke.

He was a serial womaniser, a misogynist, possibly a racist. He also had an ego without equal. Nastase was powerful with the racquet and vicious with his tongue. He walked the finest line when it came to entertaining on the court and even outshone a young McEnroe for his volatility when the two played in 1979. Two of Tennis's most enigmatic characters fought head-to-head, with Nastase turning the match into a debacle with a plethora of code violations, game penalties, and warnings for refusing to play.

The chair umpire eventually awarded the match to McEnroe with the scores 3-1. Nastase's disqualification nearly led to a riot with fans throwing beer cans on to the court and even hurling themselves on to the court.

After refusing to play on, Nastase returned to his seat and threw his towel toward the match referee. He hit the referee with his racquet and said, "It's not your business; you keep the score, okay? One more time you look at me, I will kill you."

One of the bad boys of tennis not mentioned so far is Lleyton Hewitt. He was left to last because Kyrgios has publicly stated that his former Davis Cup Captain is a wonderful support – "The only great that's ever been supportive of me the whole time has been Lleyton Hewitt... He kind of knows that I kind of do my own thing. I'm definitely the outcast of the Australian players. It sucks."

Hewitt understands Kyrgios more than anyone. Lleyton Hewitt now is staunchly revered as an Australian sporting hero, recently inducted into the International Tennis Hall of Fame. It was a long and rocky yellow brick road before he became a Wizard of Aus.

Often maligned by his own country for his over-the-top "C'MON" sock puppet celebration (sometimes used liberally after missed shots from opponents, as well as his own winners) abrasive in-your-face attitude, and backwards cap, there was much "hatin' Lleyton."

In 2001, the immature 20-year-old Hewitt had a crack at an African American linesman at the US Open for insinuating that the calls were going against him because he was white, and his opponent American James Blake was not.

This playing-the-race-card alienated tennis lovers around the world. In the same year at the French Open, Hewitt was fined $US 2415 for twice referring to tennis officials as "spastics." He even took the ATP to court, staying there was a long-running campaign to slight him after he was given a hefty fine for failing to appear at a US television interview before a tournament in Cincinnati.

As time went on and Hewitt matured, Australia grew to love him for his never-say-die attitude and burning passion for his country in the Davis Cup.

After he became the youngest World No. 1 at 20 years and eight months old, Hewitt was a Grand Slam champion at Wimbledon and the US Open before his 22nd birthday, yet sacrificed his own personal rankings to give his heart to the Australian Davis Cup team acknowledging it was his greatest honour. That won back supporters.

The future for Nick Kyrgios is that he, too, could still win the hearts and minds of all Australian audiences with efforts such as Wimbledon 2022. The crowds he attracted at the Australian Open in January proved that if Nick Kyrgios could let his tennis do the talking, Australians would be proud to call him their champion.

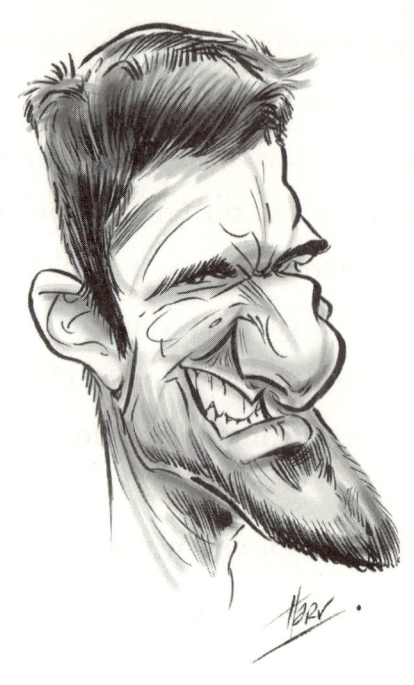

"Kyrgios is a player who has enormous talent, could be winning grand slams or fighting for the No. 1 ranking. He lacks respect for the crowd, his opponent and towards himself."

RAFAEL NADAL

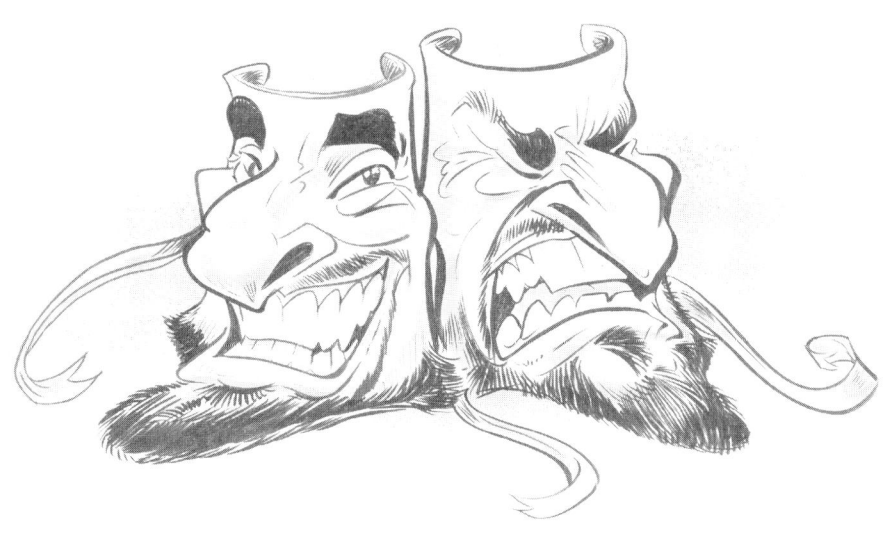

SOCK AND BUSKIN

We have a lot to thank the Greeks for. They are the forebears of so many conventions that we take for granted today. The Greeks invented democracy, mathematics, chemistry, and engineering.

In the sporting sphere, they created the ancient Olympic Games, where nude men championed sports such as javelin, discus, long-Jump, and pentathlon.

Before their time, the Greeks were also innovators in the sphere of art and artistic pursuits – sculpture, painting, architecture, and the theatre.

For many millennials or Gen Z, the term Sock and Buskin may seem obscure. If you have been to any theatre worldwide, you would have seen them.

Sock and Buskin are the names of the Comedy and Tragedy masks that have been the ancient symbol of theatre, dating back well over 2,000 years. The symbol of comedy and tragedy stems from two Greek deities. Thalia was the Muse of Comedy, while Melpomene was the Muse of Tragedy.

Sock and Buskin is a reference to the World's first-ever actors. The "sock", a thin-soled shoe, was worn by the comedian, while the tragic actors wore high-heeled boots known as a "buskin."

The "buskin" was seen as a tragic, heroic being, so the high-heeled boots were made in such a way to make them look taller.

How does this relate to Nick Kyrgios?

The riveting performance that is the life of Nick Kyrgios is a constant clash of humour and untethered anger, outrageous skill battling unbridled passion.

This is the duality of Nick Kyrgios.

Tennis to the public is theatre and Kyrgios, like him or hate him, is the sport's number one actor. His unpredictability puts bums on seats and fills the tennis coffers with dollars.

In Kyrgios's career, Sock and Buskin constantly butt heads.

At Wimbledon in 2022, Kyrgios went from screaming at his supporters' box for not cheering him enough and two seconds later hurdled down an unplayable ace that even Djokovic, one of the greatest to ever pick up a racquet, was helpless to return.

He goes from Sock to Buskin and back again in the blink of an eye, making him one of the most confounding and polarising players ever to grace a tennis court.

The tragedy of losing his first-ever Grand Slam grates against his post-game interview with English tennis legend Sue Barker.

Here he joked about Djokovic being a God and made a point of needing an extended holiday after too much tennis.

Most people take a holiday to play tennis.

From watching countless videos of Kyrgios highlights and lowlights, no game suites the Sock and Buskin reference more than his 2017 second Round Australian Open clash with Italian veteran Andreas Seppi.

After taking a 2-set lead (6-1 and 7-6), Kyrgios was serving during the third set on top of his game until he received a code violation for audible vulgarity.

This triggered an escalation, resulting in a point penalty.

While reporting on the match for *The Sydney Morning Herald*, writer Linda Pearce explained the division within Kyrgios to perfection, calling the Kyrgios in the third and fourth set as a "tortured version" of himself.

She also stated that the "extraordinary circumstances were so extreme as to be bewildering."

Fast forward to Wimbledon 2022, and Kyrgios again showed the bad Nick when he spat towards spectators who were heckling him during his first-round class with Brit Paul Jubb. He returned from losing the first set to win 3-6, 6-1, 7-5, 6-7 (3-7), 7-5.

Kyrgios gave an interesting perspective in his post-match press conference, not shying away from spitting near the crowd.

When asked if he spat toward the patrons heckling him, he dryly responded "Of course. I wouldn't be doing that to someone who was supporting me."

He added: "I've been dealing with hate and negativity for a long time, so I don't feel like I owed that person anything."

The tennis also highlighted the differences modern stars face in the 21st century, compared to maligned players in the past.

"I just think it's just a whole generation of people, on social media, feeling like they have a right to comment on every single thing with negativity, and it just carries on into real life," Kyrgios said.

"There's a fence there, and I physically can't do anything or say anything because I will get in trouble, so they just feel that they can just say anything they want.

We all watch Kyrgios, sitting on tenterhooks, wondering which theatrical mask will show itself first. Will his volatility derail his charge at the title? The Wimbledon final appearance is a testament to some new-found, and long-overdue maturity, but even in the final, he transfigured from Saint Nick to the demon Nicholas in the blink of an eye. Nick Kyrgios is like a box of chocolates. You never know what you're gonna get.

'I THOUGHT MY SHIP
HAD SAILED'
Wimbledon finalist 2022

Nick Kyrgios seemed as surprised as anyone that he reached the men's 2022 singles final at Wimbledon.

Just getting to a semi-final on the hallowed turf of The All England Club (officially the All England Lawn Tennis and Croquet Club) at Wimbledon for the Open Championship was rarefied air for him. He'd bowed out in three Grand Slam quarter-finals previously.

His best efforts until 2022 in Grand Slams were quarter-finals at Wimbledon in 2016 and 2020 and the Australian Open in 2018.

Kyrgios's run to the Wimbledon final wasn't without controversy. He reached the final thanks to the retirement through injury of Rafael Nadal from their scheduled semi-final encounter. He said he wasn't able to speak to Nadal – "I found out while I was at dinner."

"My first feeling was one of disappointment," Kyrgios said. "I had concentrated all my energies in facing him, in my game tactics, in the emotions of taking the field and everything in between. It was not easy for him to make this decision. I'm sure part of him wanted to play the game."

The walkover sparked debate about whether there should be provision for a "lucky loser" substitute.

Would there have been such vigorous debate had the recipient of the walkover been anyone else? Who knows? But it guaranteed the spotlight was firmly focussed on Kyrgios as he prepared for his biggest match on the biggest stage.

On top of that he had to contend with questions about assault allegations made against him arising from an incident the previous year. It was reported that a matter involving him was listed for a court hearing in August 2022 (it was subsequently delayed).

Why was the court action revealed at such a time? It should be noted that the alleged victim said she had nothing to do with the timing – she had reported an incident at the time, the previous December.

His legal team issued a statement. "Today's media headline that Mr Kyrgios has been 'charged' is inaccurate. At the present time, the allegations are not considered as fact by the Court, and Mr Kyrgios is not considered charged with an offence until the First Appearance.

"Until the Court formally accepts the Prosecution will be proceeding with a charge, and that the charge before the Court is to be applied to the person summoned to appear, it may be misleading to the public to describe the summons in any other manner than a formal direction to appear to face allegations, the precise nature of which is neither certain at this moment nor confirmed by either the prosecution or Mr Kyrgios.

"While Mr Kyrgios is committed to addressing any and all

allegations once clear, taking the matter seriously does not warrant any misreading of the process Mr Kyrgios is required to follow."

His Wimbledon campaign became embroiled in headlines almost daily. But the fact remained, he was playing some good – maybe even great – tennis in tight matches; four of six played on the way to the final involved tie-breakers, which he won. His luck ran out in the final when he lost a tie-break in the fourth set to hand Djokovic a seventh Wimbledon title and 21st Grand Slam title.

The struggle began in Kyrgios's first match against British No. 8, wild card entry and local hero Paul Jubb, a feel-good story of having risen from council estate orphan to the turf of the world's premier tournament.

The match could have gone either way, just a couple of points the difference. It took Kyrgios more than three hours to overcome the Brit, his 30 aces and 67 winners being the difference. He won a tense five-setter, dropping two sets.

There were some Kyrgios moments; he complained about the slowness of the court. He called a line judge a "snitch" for reporting him for foul language and later demanded a spectator be removed. He was accused of spitting in the direction of a spectator after the match ended. The media described the behaviour as a meltdown.

Kyrgios's second round match against Filip Krajinovic (Serbia) was a subdued affair, taking just three sets, but produced a moment of levity in the interviews afterward. "I just wanted to remind everyone that I'm pretty good," Kyrgios said with a blank expression. That got a big laugh.

"I love that you just said that with a deadpan face, as well," the interviewer said. "No smile?"

Kyrgios stayed cool. "Nah," he said.

Anyone who thought there'd be no more controversy was mistaken – there was more, notably in the third-round encounter with Stefanos Tsitsipas of Greece, which led to big fines dished out to both players.

Yet, several commentators voted it the best match of the tournament, as chaotic as it was.

Kyrgios demanded Tsitsipas be defaulted for hitting a ball into the stands, just missing a female spectator. He threatened a sit-down protest after Tsitsipas only received a code violation. Tsitsipas also appeared to try to hit Kyrgios with a ball.

"You can't hit a ball into a crowd and hit someone and not be defaulted," Kyrgios yelled at the chair umpire repeatedly while pointing out that Novak Djokovic was defaulted from the 2020 US Open for hitting a linesperson with a ball.

"I would like to speak to a supervisor. I'm not playing until I speak to a supervisor," Kyrgios demanded. "Bring out more supervisors. I'm not done. Bring them all out."

He was ignored by the officials. Kyrgios also called the chair umpire a disgrace and received a code violation after being reported by a linesman for swearing.

Tsitsipas complained to the chair umpire, "this isn't tennis" and copped a point penalty for smacking a return off a Kyrgios underarm serve into the scoreboard.

After dropping the first set in a tiebreaker, Kyrgios won the next three including the last, also in a tiebreaker.

He didn't drop serve all night, saving all five break points he faced, and put away 14 aces. There was some concern among his supporters when he fell awkwardly in the opening game of the fourth set and clutched his hip.

But he recovered to defeat Tsitsipas for the fourth time in as many clashes.

"I felt like the favourite coming in. I played him a couple of weeks ago (and won), but I knew it was going to be a tough match," Kyrgios said.

"He's a hell of a player and it was a hell of a match. I'm just super happy to be through.

"He was getting frustrated at times — it's a frustrating sport. You all think you can play, but it's very frustrating."

Kyrgios had a message for his critics: "Everywhere I go its full stadiums. The media love to write that I'm bad for the sport, but clearly not," he said.

But some good tennis was in the offing as he moved forward in the draw, showdowns looming with Nadal and Djokovic. His record against both was good; in six matches with Nadal the results stood at 3-3 and he had beaten Djokovic in their two previous matches.

First there was 20-year-old Brandon Nakashima, the pair were closely ranked with the American at No. 49 and Kyrgios at No. 45.

Kyrgios struggled to time the ball early, apparently suffering from shoulder pain. In the eighth game of the first set, he exercised the shoulder and was in some discomfort. In the second set he resorted to some painkillers.

The shoulder remained a concern as he received treatment between changes of serve. But he took the second set reasonably comfortably and clinched the third in a tiebreaker.

Losing the fourth was a surprise that had Australian commentator Todd Woodbridge saying Kyrgios "tanked" (gave up) in the last game to lose it.

Whatever happened in the fourth set, Kyrgios was back on song in the decider. After breaking Nakashima for a 2-1 lead, he sealed a succession of games emphatically – an ace out wide for 3-1, a cross-court backhand winner for a second break, and a second-serve ace for 5-1. He closed it out with another flurry of winners.

Kyrgios said he hadn't been worried about being taken to five sets: "My five-set record's pretty good; I've never lost a five-set match here," he said, having a 6-0 record in deciding sets at Wimbledon after he wrapped up the match.

Asked about his shoulder, Kyrgios said he had "played a lot of tennis in the past month" so there was some concern as he prepared to face Cristian Garin in the quarter-final, his first appearance there since 2014.

Asked if he was looking forward to the clash, Kyrgios said he was looking forward to "a glass of wine."

Possibly realising what was at stake, Kyrgios was more subdued and focussed in his clash with the Chilean, at least until a flare-up on match point, which had to be replayed after the umpire overruled a linesperson's call.

Kyrgios was emotional after the victory, fighting back tears.

Then in his on-court interview, he revealed he had thought he may never make it past a quarter-final.

"I just never thought I would be at a semi-final of a Grand Slam. Honestly, I thought my ship had sailed," he said.

He was to face Raphael Nadal, possibly with some hope having a 3-4 record against the Spaniard even though he had lost at Wimbledon to him in the second round in 2019.

A shock was to come. Nadal said he was conceding a walkover after being unable to serve properly during practice. He suffered an abdominal tear.

As disappointing as that was for all, it propelled Kyrgios into the men's championship final, the first Australian to get there in 19 years.

Nadal said he'd carried the muscle injury through the first week of the championships before aggravating it during his five-set quarter-final win over American Taylor Fritz.

"As everybody saw yesterday, I have been suffering with the pain in abdominal. I know something was not okay there," he said.

Nick Kyrgios became the first unseeded man to reach a major final since Jo-Wilfried Tsonga at the 2008 Australian Open, the first Australian man to reach a major final since Lleyton Hewitt at the

2005 Australian Open, and the first unseeded or Australian man to reach the Wimbledon final since Mark Philippoussis in 2003.

The Kyrgios path to the final at Wimbledon:

Round of 128: defeated Paul Jubb (England) 3-6, 6-1, 7-5, 6-7 (3-7 tiebreak), 7-5.

Round of 64: defeated Filip Krajinovic (Serbia) 6-2, 6-3, 6-1.

Round of 32: defeated Stefanos Tsitsipas (4th seed, Greece) 6-4, 6-3, 7-6 (9-7 tiebreak).

Round of 16: defeated Brandon Nakashima (US) 4-6, 6-4, 7-6 (7-2 tiebreak) 3-6, 6-2.

Quarter-final: defeated Christian Garin (Chile) 6-4, 6-3, 7-6 (7-3 tiebreak).

Semi-final: defeated Raphael Nadal (Spain) walkover.

GAME, SET, MATCH AND CHAMPIONSHIP

On July 10, on a centre court where the temperature passed 35 degrees Celsius, Novak Djokovic kept his cool to seal the Open Championship 4-6, 6-3, 6-4, 7-6 (7/3 tiebreak).

He had a scare early, dropping the first set. But the top-seed accounted for the unseeded Australian playing in his first Grand Slam final, in just on three hours.

The Kyrgios experience was over, despite a roaring start. His 30 aces were not enough to overcome the Serb whose first-serve success rate was 82% compared to Kyrgios's 70% although the Australian got more first serves in play and hit more winners (62-46).

The win gave Djokovic his seventh Wimbledon title, his 21st Grand Slam title moving him to just one behind the record of Rafael Nadal. Only Roger Federer had won more Wimbledon titles, eight.

After taking the first set and showing great composure, Kyrgios seemed to lose his way. While he remonstrated with his support team – "Why do you stop [cheering]? Why? Why do you? Say something!" Djokovic remained cool in the cauldron of Centre Court.

Djokovic continued to press while Kyrgios became even more frustrated, firing at the chair umpire about a spectator.

"There is no bigger occasion than a Wimbledon final... you should kick her out."

That's pretty much where the Australian's tilt at glory ended, Djokovic taking the third set comfortably and clinching the title in a tiebreaker in the fourth after Kyrgios had managed to hold his serve to get to 6-6.

Some key points from the final:

Djokovic maintained his unbeaten streak at Wimbledon. He had won 28 straight matches, clinching four straight titles. His last defeat was a walkover to Thomas Berdych in 2017. He had the fourth-longest streak behind Bjorn Borg (41), Roger Federer (40), Pete Sampras (31).

At 35 years 49 days, Djokovic became the second oldest man in the Open Era to win the Wimbledon singles title – after Federer, who won the title in 2017 aged 35 years 342 days.

Djokovic had now won nine Grand Slam titles since turning 30 years old. No one has more. Nadal was the nearest competitor with 8 titles. Djokovic now had a 21-11 record in the Grand Slam finals.

Djokovic continued the dominance of the Big Three in majors; He, Nadal and Federer having won 63 of the 76 majors played since Wimbledon in 2003.

Kyrgios finished the grass-court season with the most match victories, 12 tour-level matches on grass in 2022. Djokovic won seven, all at Wimbledon.

Australia's drought for a Grand Slam winner stretched to 20 years. Lleyton Hewitt was the last major champion – Wimbledon in 2002

The loss meant Kyrgios had not won a singles title in nearly three years. His last trophy was 2019 in Washington.

The result gave Djokovic a 27-9 win/loss record for 52 weeks (two titles) and Kyrgios a 17-11 win/loss record for the same period.

HOW THE MATCH WAS PLAYED

Novak Djokovic		Nick Kyrgios
15	aces	30
7	double faults	7
63%	first serves in	73%
83%	win first serve	70%
61%	win second serve	53%
60%	net points won	56%
50%	break points won	17%
29%	receiving points won	19%
46	winners	62
17	unforced errors	33
132	total points won	112

It was Djokovic's seventh Wimbledon title and 21st career major singles title. He became the fifth man in the era of Open championships to post a streak of at least four consecutive titles at one major.

It was his 32nd men's singles major final, passing the record he had jointly held with Roger Federer. Djokovic also became the first player (male or female) to win 80 matches at all four majors with his win in the first-round.

After the match

There were plenty of fans feeling a little empty after Kyrgios's defeat, even though very few would have expected him to win.

He did win praise for getting there and taking a set off Djokovic. He had plenty of supporters as he took to the court, many in Australia.

But it is a measure of who Nick Kyrgios is that one of his treasured messages of support came from someone called Stormzy, to whom he replied, "Bro I did my best."

The exchange may have mystified many social media watchers. For the uninitiated, Stormzy – born Michael Ebenezer Kwadjo Omari Owuo Jr – is a British rapper.

He sent Kyrgios a video message before the final: "Nick, we're rooting for you my boy. Come on, I'm here for you bro, yeah."

Later, in the US where he was contesting the hardcourt swing leading up the US Open, Kyrgios conceded he had struggled to get past his four-set loss to Djokovic but was on his way.

"It was really hard, it took me a while to get over that loss," he said.

"Ever since I picked up a racquet that's always been a goal that I was told – Wimbledon final, Wimbledon championship.

"That's the highest accolade you can achieve, and I was so

close I could almost taste it.

"I feel like I've done everything I can to bounce back. I've been training hard, my body's feeling good, serving great so we'll see how it goes."

WHAT THE WIMBLEDON COMBATANTS SAID:

NOVAK DJOKOVIC

Nick, you'll be back. Not just in Wimbledon but in many finals. You showed why you are one of the best players in the world. Congrats to you and your team. I wish you all the best, man. I really think you are an amazing talent. I never thought I'm going to say so many nice things about you, considering the relationship! OK, it's officially a bromance! Hopefully this is the start of a wonderful friendship. Let's start with dinner and drinks and we will see.

I'm lost words for what this trophy means. It has always been and always will be the most special tournament. Realising a childhood dream in winning this trophy. Every year it gets more meaningful, I am really blessed. The most special court in the world. I am extremely happy and grateful to be here.

NICK KYRGIOS

Yeah he is a bit of a god, I'm not going to lie. I thought I played well. First of all congratulations to Novak and your team, you've won this Championships that many times I don't even know any more.

Obviously to all the ball kids, the umpires, I know we have a tough relationship at times so thanks for putting up with it. And [thanks] to the crowd, it has been an amazing couple of weeks for me personally.

I'm so tired honestly. Myself, my team, we're all exhausted. We've played so much tennis. I'm really happy with this result and maybe one day I'll be here again but I don't know about that.

NEXT STOP

On the Sunday night after the Wimbledon final Kyrgios hit the Dolce nightclub in ritzy High St, Kensington, with girlfriend Costeen, sister Halimah and the rest of his entourage.

He then headed home to the Bahamas to soak up some sunshine with girlfriend Costeen. It was a long trip – the pair had to sleep on the floor at Toronto airport while waiting for their connection, and for their luggage to be found.

When they reached home, it was time to relax. Social media was dotted with pictures of the pair enjoying beach life.

The next tournament – and the lead-up to the next Slam – was two weeks away.

The US Open was at the end of August, his chance perhaps for that first Slam.

THE VIEW FROM COURTSIDE

Maybe, just maybe, Nick Kyrgios is growing up? One of his staunchest critics, Channel Nine's leading sports reporter Tony Jones was in England covering Wimbledon for the first time.

Channel Nine was getting its money's worth from Jones, as he continued to anchor Nine Melbourne's evening sporting bulletin at 6 pm, often from centre court. He then did live crosses for Nine's *Today* show, often at the stadium at midnight, and still managed to squeeze in enough time for live crosses for Melbourne radio station 3AW.

Jones's role as the senior journalist at Wimbledon for Channel Nine gave him a unique perspective on Kyrgios.

Once regarding Kyrgios as a "foul-mouthed little brat" after a verbal stoush with a chair umpire at the Miami Open in 2019, Jones, like many, admired the outrageous potential Kyrgios possesses yet rightfully criticised him for the all-too-common childish antics on the court as he abused the chair umpire.

Jump forward to Wimbledon 2022 and it would appear that Jones's opinion of Kyrgios has been tempered after numerous interviews with him post-match in London.

Have the views of the veteran journalist softened, or is Nick becoming less abrasive?

Maybe a little from column A and a little from column B.

Author Sam Harvey asked Tony about what he saw of Kyrgios at Wimbledon.

Q: *What was the public reaction to Kyrgios in London? What did they think of him?*

Jones: What did the public think of Nick at Wimbledon? Well, the Poms, they just couldn't get enough of him. I think they were disappointed on the occasions when he just went out and played tennis and didn't have any tantrums, didn't have any sort of, you know, blow-ups or anything like that. Didn't yell at his box and just got on with playing tennis. In fact, I remember as we were leaving one of the courts, one British journalist said to another British journalist, "well, there's our story for tomorrow, 'Kyrgios makes tennis boring'." They absolutely loved him, from the old Wimbledon members right down to those who camped out in tents for two nights, just in the hope of getting a ticket. Yet I'd read the papers back here and read the letters to the editor, they smashed him; you couldn't get poles apart in terms of his polarising nature.

Q: *He was treated like a rockstar in Melbourne during the 2022 Australian Open where he won the doubles title with best mate Thanasi Kokkinakis; did he get that sort of treatment at Wimbledon?*

Jones: Yeah. Oh my God. It was unbelievable. The atmosphere – it was actually like being at a rock concert... and I've been to a few; it was like a WWE night at Rod Laver arena (laughs). It was almost like one of those. It was like something that you've never seen at a tennis match before. It was phenomenal.

I know we got close to it in the Australian summer at Kia Arena with the Special Ks.

However, this wasn't a double act. This was Nick and Nick alone. The Kyrgios game vs. Stefanos Tsitsipas was phenomenal. I don't know how you actually replicate that, it was off the charts and then the darkness came, and they stopped the match, suspending it for several minutes. Then they closed the roof and turned the lights on. At this point it became surreal. It took on a whole new atmosphere. Again, it was just absolutely volcanic in there.

Q: *Kyrgios has stated that he receives no support from past greats. You have interviewed past greats like Rod Laver and John Newcombe, do they have an opinion on Nick?*

Jones: They all agree that if he found a new composure within himself, he could be anything. He could win tournaments all around the world. He's just got to knuckle down. And I think therein lies the frustration with guys like Newcombe and Laver, Margaret Court as well. They're fans, but they know that he lets himself down badly with his explosions on the court.

Everyone concedes he's a very, very gifted tennis player. They're in no doubt about that.

He could easily be top five, he could be top five by the middle of next year if he wanted to be, but he doesn't want to be, because he doesn't like tennis. He's not going to get a coach because, by his own admission, he is not going to put anyone through that (laughs).

I mean, one of the things he would have to do is get off social media for starters, he's addicted to it, and it doesn't do him a lot of favours.

Q: *2019 was a bad year for Kyrgios, he was acting up on the court and playing badly. Do you think he has improved as a competitor and has grown up a bit?*

Jones: Well, he has grown up and I think there were a couple of turning points. One, the bushfires in Australia; that's when he really took a lead role and helped create the "Rally Relief", where so much money was raised through tennis for the bushfire victims.* I think he really stepped up there and we saw a different side of Nick. I also think, through Covid, he became a bit of a moral crusader and he was taking aim at Novak for the bare-chested parties at the height of Covid and a couple of others who stepped out of line. We've certainly seen instances where he's acted with maturity. He's grown up. I mean, he's still only 26 or 27 and any psychologist will tell you that the male brain doesn't mature fully until well after that.

*(Kyrgios with the help of other Tennis stars such as Roger Federer raised $4,826,014 for the bushfire victims in Australia).

Q: *I started writing about how Kyrgios shares many similarities with* Happy Gilmore. *He's so talented at one sport yet looks like he'd rather be playing basketball, or computer games.*

Jones: That's one of the things that we spoke about just before the final. We did a one-on-one interview and he said that if he was to win against Novak (Djokovic), then what else was there to achieve? He said: "I've been brought up my whole life being told Wimbledon is the absolute ultimate. So, if I win Wimbledon there's nothing else to achieve. There are no more hurdles to overcome."

I said, "What are you talking about. Retirement?" And he said, "Well, why not? I've got nothing else to prove to anyone."

And I said, "Are you doing an Ash Barty on us? He said, "Well, I can't do that because I can't do anything else. I'm not good at anything else. I'm pretty good at basketball, and I'm good at Nintendo, but outside of that, I've got nothing" (laughs).

So, it would've been really interesting if he had won (Wimbledon), and he could've won and should have won, whether he would've actually gone through with that (retirement) and can I tell you, I suspect he would have.

Q: *Where to now for him? What does the next five years look like for Nick? After his maiden Wimbledon final, there's still so many people that don't know what he's going to do in the future.*

Jones: Because he doesn't know, and if you were to ask him today and ask him tomorrow, the answers would be completely different. He doesn't know himself and therein lies the great mystery that is Nick. I mean, if he had his game and Pat Rafter's character, he would be one of the most marketable sports people in the world. He could write his own cheque for anything. He would be rolling in money, but it's not important to him, and nor is it important for him to be liked, I think. That honesty is a little endearing actually. He doesn't care. I mean he says time and time again, any publicity's good publicity. When I think back to some of the media conferences and the one-on-ones that we did, I got the sense after the combative media conferences that he was genuinely hurt.

Q: *What was your opinion on him? Did that change since you spent time with him?*

Jones: He's a great kid. Yeah. Look, I was really surprised because I was one of his harshest critics, but then sitting down, and I'm not going pretend that I got to know him per se. All I can do is judge on, you know, the little bits of conversation that we had prior to each interview and the way he conducted himself through those interviews, keeping in mind those interviews are conducted not long after he has come off the court. He's just been through a full media, often combative media conference. Invariably there's argy-bargy and then he's got another one to do with me! He was always very polite. He was not uppity. He was a good young kid and I walked away from there, probably, a fan, and I now genuinely hope he does well.

I just wish he would eradicate certain parts of his game, i.e. abusing his own box, which just doesn't sit comfortably. I find it really embarrassing.

Q: *It's just amazing how a little switch can flick, and he loses concentration, loses focus. Do you know if he's doing any mindfulness training or anything. Does he work on this sort of thing?*

Jones: I don't know to be honest. It was quiet glaring when they were training side by side before the final (Kyrgios and Djokovic). Novak Djokovic has got a team, which is like a small army, and then on the next court, you've got Nick with his small outpost, his sister and one of his mates just throwing balls back to him. It was a very lean operation. He travels lean, works lean. It reminded me of that show *Entourage**; he's just got his mates with him, and they're all having an absolute hoot.

*(*Entourage* is a TV series about a Hollywood hotshot known as Vincent Chase whose brother (his manager) and his friends help him navigate his wild life in Hollywood as Chase soars into stardom).

Q: *That reminds me of scene in the film* Talladega Nights *when Ricky Bobby (played by Will Ferrell) makes his comeback, and because he has no sponsors, his team prints a big "You" on the front of the car. Nick plays for himself, this is his movie isn't it?*

Jones: Excuse me for name dropping but you've reminded me of something. I actually asked Rebel Wilson that question (Nick Kyrgios's life is a movie script?). The day or the day before the Wimbledon men's final. I said to her, "It would make a good script for a movie, the life of Nick Kyrgios...What type of movie would it be?"

Rebel said, "Oh, it'd definitely be a drama, and I think it will also be quite funny really. *Kyrgios – the Movie!*"

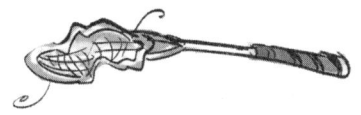

In summary, like many others, Tony Jones hopes that Nick can be the Grand Slam champion his prodigious talent suggests he could be.

Not everyone will have the luxury of meeting and interviewing Nick Kyrgios, like Tony Jones has, and being charmed by his affable nature and honest sense of humour. The rest of us have to be swayed by a yet-to-be-convinced media, especially in his home country of Australia.

It is clear that some critics will never be won over, no matter how many Grand Slams he might win. He has done his dash with them, his antics have alienated them, and they will never support him.

It is also clear, from Tony's observation, that a younger generation of tennis supporters think he is the earthquake that the staid and curmudgeonly tennis establishment people needs, to rock them to their core.

It is also clear, from past quotes, that Nick also sees himself this way.

"I know what I bring to the sport," he said after a match at Wimbledon. "I'm one of the most important people in tennis. There's nothing to investigate about this, it's, it's a fact. I've overcome many obstacles in my life. I'm very proud to be here and play this way. It's a dream come true to be at Wimbledon."

Nick in his post-match interview after defeating Brit Paul Jubb in the first round of Wimbledon 2022 (3-6 6-1 7-5 6-7 (3-7) 7-5) said: "I'm extremely confident in myself. All the challenges

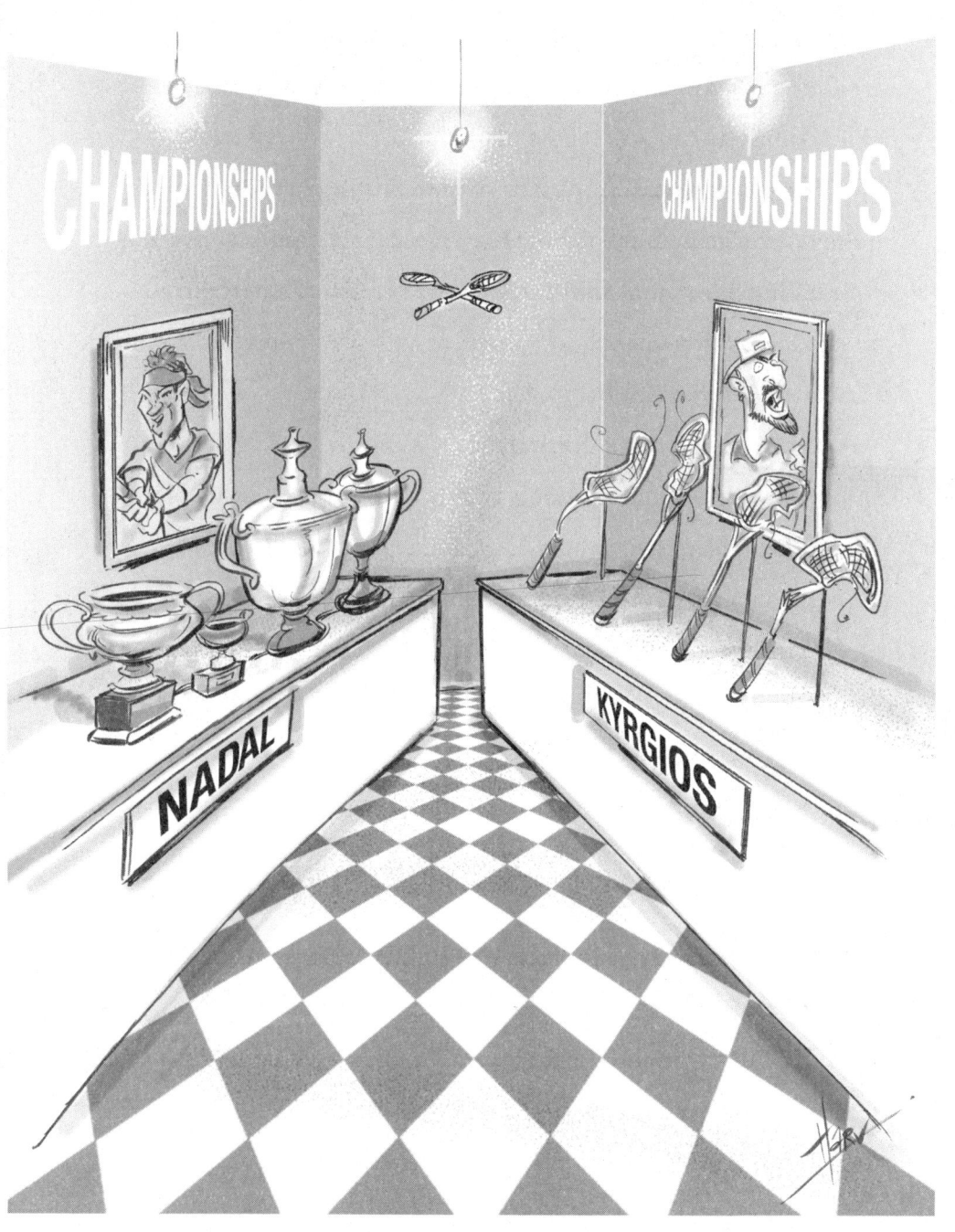

I've overcome in my life. Proud to be up here and doing it my own way. Being able to produce tennis like that at Wimbledon, it's a dream come true for any tennis player."

This new, maturing Kyrgios has the physical endurance of a Djokovic that has eluded him in the past. Has the strong precise shot-making of a Nadal and has a little bit of that Federer magic and audacious shot-making. Yet he doesn't have the temperament of any of them. Not really.

Surely we can hope the success at Wimbledon stokes the fire. Can Nick Kyrgios hold it all together long enough to win a Slam?

TAKING DOWN THE WORLD'S BEST

World rankings don't mean all that much to Nick Kyrgios when he faces an opponent, whether it be the World No.1 or a qualifier.

At the US Open in August 2022, Kyrgios, ranked No. 32 in the world on the men's tour, became the first player in 35 years to beat a World No. 1 twice in the same year.

In fact, the higher the ranking, the more Kyrgios seems to rise to the occasion. Russian Daniil Medvedev, who became World No. 1 in February 2022, could testify to that; he was on the losing end to the Australian in August and September.

Kyrgios had claimed a number of Top 10 scalps, including Tsitsipas, Ruud, Rublev and Nadal, the latter by walkover at Wimbledon.

Kyrgios excelled on grass in 2022, reaching the semi-finals back-to-back in Stuttgart and Halle.

World No. 6 Stefanos Tsitsipas fell to him in Halle, the Greek's third loss in four meetings with Kyrgios, and he lost again at Wimbledon.

The Halle win over Tsitsipas moved Kyrgios to third on the list of active male players with the most wins against top-10 players without ever breaking into the top-10 themselves.

Other members of the top tier – Andrey Rublev and Casper Ruud – also were Kyrgios victims in 2022.

He went into Wimbledon in June confident he could beat the best: "I've played top-10 players in the world this year and made them look pretty ordinary," he said.

"I know where my game's at. I know if I'm feeling confident, I'm playing well, I'm able to just light it up kind of whenever I want."

Medvedev twice felt the force of a Kyrgios takedown, first in Montreal and next, more significantly, in the US Open in New York; that loss would likely cost him top spot in the world rankings.

The Russian may have been underdone when he arrived in the US for the North American swing, not having played since June and having to miss Wimbledon because of the All England Club's ban on players from Russia and Belarus in response to Russia's invasion of Ukraine (there was no such ban from the ATP from its events, although players from there were not able to appear under the flag of their country).

That didn't mean Kyrgios's victories were any less impressive. Kyrgios took him down 6-7(1), 6-4, 6-2 in Montreal as his sparkling run of form that started at Wimbledon a month earlier continued in the US.

Medvedev was tipped to do well in New York, and things went his way comfortably through the first three rounds. Then he faced Kyrgios.

Victory for the Australian wasn't as straightforward as in Montreal – four sets this time, but some more amazing tennis.

Their clash in the US Open began with a marathon first set, Kyrgios eventually prevailing 7-6 in a tiebreak (13-11).

Kyrgios then dropped the second set 3-6 but finished the Russian off 6-3, 6-2.

The victory was Kyrgios's fourth over Medvedev in five career meetings and his third over a reigning World No. 1. (He shocked the tennis world in 2014 when he defeated Raphael Nadal at Wimbledon).

After a relatively quiet start (for Kyrgios that is) to the North American hard-court swing, some of the on-court antics returned in Montreal – complaining about a high bounce, hitting a ball into the stands drawing a warning, and bickering with his player box about support in tight moments.

But he remained focussed enough to take care of Medvedev in two hours.

Before he left the court, Kyrgios wrote a message on a TV camera lens.

"Be strong Ma," he wrote to his mother who was in hospital back home in Canberra.

"It's hard to be away from Australia now. My mum is in hospital, my dad hasn't been very well," he said.

"People only see me winning, losing, throwing a racquet. They do not really understand the challenges that we players face in our personal lives."

At Flushing Meadows at the beginning of September, Medvedev was defending champion. Kyrgios had come from

Cincinnati where he bowed out with barely a whimper in straight sets to big-hitting American Taylor Fritz, 3-6, 2-6 , in less than an hour in the round of 32. He appeared to have trouble with a knee that increased speculation about his prospects in the US Open.

But there was no evidence of a problem as he smashed his way through the first three rounds to face Medvedev again.

Kyrgios proved his victory over the Russian in Montreal was no accident. His tennis at Flushing Meadows was brilliant at times.

"It was an amazing match, I played really well. I've been playing amazing. What a place to do it," he said.

"I'm still trying to figure it out, I'm trying to work hard every day, make every session count. Before I would be out every night, now I have a great girlfriend. My team, it's all my team, I'm working really hard I hope I can keep it going.

"I don't want to let them down, I've been on the road for four months, we all have families we want to see, I want to make this count."

The win at Flushing Meadows would move Kyrgios into the top 20.

The Australian had not been deeper than the round of 64 in the US Open. His victory over Medvedev put him into the last eight and had commentators daring to think he could go all the way.

For Medvedev, the writing was on the wall at Montreal, despite Kyrgios's failure to progress at Cincinnati.

Kyrgios lost the first set in Montreal in a tie-break after he had two set points on the Medvedev serve at 5-4 but could not convert. He broke Medvedev's serve to start the second set and went on to level the match, then take the decider although Medvedev had two break points in the second game.

The first set at Flushing Meadows also went to a tie-break, Kyrgios prevailing this time.

"There's so many little things that we have to deal with on a day-to-day basis and also try to beat players like Daniil Medvedev. It seems impossible," Kyrgios said after victory in Montreal. "It takes a lot of work. That's for sure."

"I feel like I'm just playing for a lot more than myself now. I look at today, I'm in Montreal, centre court, one of the most beautiful courts in the world against Medvedev.

"I would be kind of selfish to not go out there and try to give the crowd a good performance, myself a good performance, my team a good performance, everyone watching.

"I feel like if I didn't show up today, I'd be doing a lot of people a disservice. That's what's sport needs, the sport needs matchups like this."

He was asked about his fitness. "At this late stage of the year, everyone suffers a little from something, we are not quite fresh. I'm at the stage where I get up in the morning a little tired, my warm-ups are a little shorter," he said.

"I try to do the minimum to preserve my energy for the game. I warmed up for 10 minutes today and then went back to go to the physio's table. It's very important for me to have my physio full time with me right now. I couldn't do it last year because of

Covid. I struggled to manage my body. Now I have two or three hours of work a day. I'm able to handle the post-match better than I've ever been able to.

"I am in a good state of mind, very positive. My partner helps me stay positive. My team surrounds me and knows that mentally, it starts there. If I get up in the morning thinking I don't want to play, with a slow mind, I'd necessarily feel physically soft too. I have to stay positive mentally, think about my good series right now, and capitalise on those successes."

Kyrgios began 2022 ranked No. 39 and blew out to No. 137 in February. Had rankings been available from Wimbledon results he would have gone on to the North American swing as World No. 15, instead of No. 37 which was still his highest ranking in two-and-a-half years.

He wasn't particularly interested in the rankings of opponents.

"I don't go in looking at the rankings, just the guy in front of me," he said after defeating Medvedev.

"I had a clean objective today; play a lot of serve and volley and execute better."

As Medvedev left the court in Montreal, some fans chanted "loser" at him. Kyrgios defended the Russian with a Twitter post after he became aware of the incident when footage was posted on social media, criticising "disgusting" fans for not showing respect to the world No. 1. "This is the best we have in the sport, fans need to show some respect." he tweeted.

HALF DOZEN OF THE GREATEST MATCHES

For almost the last 20 years men's tennis has been dominated by three individuals, "The Joker", Serbian Novak Djokovic, the "King of Clay" Rafael Nadal, and the "Swiss Maestro" Roger Federer.

This isn't hyperbole: we will never see a period of such dominance by three individuals in one sport again. What the Big 3 have done for the tennis and sport in general, is hard to fathom.

Since the Australian Open in 2003, they have won 63 of the 78 Grand Slam Titles, more than 80%!

Since Kyrgios turned pro in 2013, there have been 38 men's singles Grand Slam tournaments, with the Big 3 winning 30 of them. Sometimes it feels as though they are just waxing titles between themselves.

Here's a little-known fact about Nick Kyrgios.

He is only the third player in history to defeat all three.

Of all the players to have stepped on to a court while these leviathans lurked across the net only Kyrgios, Slovakian Dominik Hrbaty and fellow Australian and mentor Lleyton Hewitt have left the court victorious at least once!

There is an important distinction here though. Hrbaty and Hewitt defeated the Big 3 when they were teenagers before they had won any Grand Slam Titles. Kyrgios defeated Nadal at 19 years of age at Wimbledon in 2014. Ten months later, he defeated

Federer at the Madrid Open in Spain and then defeated Djokovic twice in a fortnight in 2017, at the Mexican Open and Indian Wells Open in the US.

Nick Kyrgios, for a player that hasn't won a single Grand Slam title, has gifted the world with memorable matches that will be written and remembered in the annals of tennis history.

These are his six best.

2021 Australian Open 2R vs. Ugo Humbert
5-7, 6-4, 3-6, 7-6 (7-2), 6-4.

Kicking off his 2021 Australian Open campaign with a 6-4, 6-4, 6-4 victory over Spanish qualifier Frederico Silva, Nick Kyrgios moved on to the second round to face World No. 29, Frenchman Ugo Humbert.

This match was a Kyrgios special. It had smashed racquets, shouting at the chair umpire, a boisterous home crowd, and a miraculous comeback from Australia's greatest showman. This match showed the duality of Nick Kyrgios more than any. When Kyrgios knows he's on his last legs with nothing to lose, we see the best of Nick. 2-1 sets down heading into the third, Kyrgios found himself struggling against Humbert, who was serving for the match at 5-4 in the fourth set. Kyrgios dug his heels in, saved two match points, and sent the fourth set into a tiebreaker.

Early on in his career, Kyrgios earned respect for his skill, yet had many critical of his inability to concentrate late in games and play out five sets. (Kyrgios lost to Italian Andreas Seppi in the second round of the 2017 Australian Open after winning the first two sets 6-1, 7-6, 4-6, 2-6, 8-10).

Feeding off what he described as an "intense" atmosphere, Kyrgios came to life in the fourth set tie-breaker. After Humbert pushed Kyrgios deep into the box with a soaring double-hand backhand, Kyrgios plucked the ball out of the depths with a scintillating forehand drive down the line. He then began to utilise the pace of Humbert's left-hand serves.

Kyrgios used power to punish his double backhand and finished the tiebreaker with an ace winning 7-2, with the set lasting 51 minutes. In the fifth and final set, the Australian and the Frenchman traded blows before Kyrgios broke away. The coup de gras – a powerful wide serve that caught the line. Kyrgios fell to his knees having produced one of Tennis's great escapes.

2015 MADRID OPEN 2R vs. ROGER FEDERER
6-7 (2-7), 7-6 (7-5), 7-6 (14-12).

The day the Great Swiss Maestro was humbled by a 20-year-old from Canberra.

Ranked 35 in the World, Nick Kyrgios reached superhuman levels breaking Federer in the first set then produced an ace masterclass and pounded the Swiss great with baseline winners for the second top-five win of his career. Federer, ranked No. 2 in the world at the time, said he had a "horrible performance on return of serve."

Further: "As the match went on, it got so bad that I just

couldn't get into decent positions on the return. He's got a wonderful serve, good potential..."

After fighting back from a break down, Federer won the first set and dominated the tiebreak 7-2. Kyrgios then broke Federer to get back on serve before racing out to a 5-0 tie-break lead, keeping his cool and winning his first set. The two then traded blows on the clay court before facing the match's third and final tie-break. Like two chess greats, the master and the apprentice exchanged points in the tie-break, with Federer saving five match points before Kyrgios broke away, finishing the tie-break 14-12.

Kyrgios described the experience: "This is definitely the greatest win over my career so far. It doesn't really feel real at the moment. I didn't really feel as if I was playing out there. It almost felt like I was watching."

Kyrgios hit 22 aces throughout the 157-minute match and won 79% of his first serves.

2017 Mexican Open QF vs. Novak Djokovic
7-6 (11-9), 7-5 &
2017 Indian Falls Open vs. Novak Djokovic
6-4, 7-6.

In the space of two weeks, Nick Kyrgios defeated the great Novak Djokovic twice, becoming the first player in five years to knock the Serbian off in back-to-back tournaments and the first player in eight years to knock him off twice in eight years.

Kyrgios first defeated Djokovic at the Mexican Open. Only

21 at the time, Kyrgios fired down 25 aces compared to Djokovic's two and won 85% of his first serves.

Djokovic used the court's space, particularly early in the first set, going up 5-4 before Kyrgios fought back, mirroring Djokovic's style and pushing it into a tie-break. With the crowd on Djokovic's side, Kyrgios's serving game came to the fore when he was 6-7 down, asserting his power. At one point Djokovic did "the splits" leaping for a return and was lucky to avoid damaging himself. The Serbian fought back hard, reaching set-point at 9-8 before the "Joker" uncharacteristically faulted twice, gifting Kyrgios the first set. The second set was similarly poised with scores at 6-5 before Kyrgios blasted Djokovic off his feet with pace, soaring to 40-0 before dispatching the World No. 2 with a brutal forehand.

The following week, the two faced off again at Indian Wells for the BNP Paribas Open in California.

Again, Kyrgios had the upper hand, winning in straight sets. He sent down 14 aces to 2 and won 86% of first serves. In bright yellow shoes and a green shirt, the calm Djokovic and the bubbling Kyrgios traded blows before the young Australian stepped up to reach 5-4. He outplayed Djokovic, winning the first set, before the usually cool-headed Serbian smashed his racquet into the hard court. During the second set, Kyrgios was up 40-30 with the score 5-5. Djokovic worked the then 21-year-old around, running him all over the court. He took the lead 6-5. With Kyrgios now serving, he aced the World No. 2 to send it into another tiebreak. With the "Joker" getting increasingly frustrated, Kyrgios lifted to the moment and won the set 6-3, and the match.

2020 AUSTRALIAN OPEN 3R VS. KAREN KHACHANOV
6-2, 7-6 (7-5), 6-7 (6-8), 6-7 (7-9), 7-6 (10-8).

In an epic match that went for four hours and 28 minutes, Kyrgios again looked like he would lose his cool and give up his two-set advantage over Russian Karen Khachanov.

Yet again, Kyrgios was his own worst enemy. The volcanic star turned what was a breezy two-set lead into something out of Stanley Kubrick's *The Shining*. He had the pro-Kyrgios crowd sweating as Khachanov fought back to take the third set 6-7 (6-8) and the fourth set 6-7 (7-9).

Kyrgios managed to keep his cool, even though in discomfort with a nasty hip injury.

His temperament was tested when chair umpire Renaud Lichtenstein gave him a time violation after Kyrgios made sure the ball boy didn't touch his bloodied towel after suffering a nasty cut on his hand. (Kyrgios cut his hand after hitting a miraculous winner while falling to the ground, with the score 4-4).

"There is blood all over the towel and I told the ball kid not to touch it. Take it back then. Why do I get a time violation, my hand is bleeding?" Kyrgios said.

As the scorching sun set, Khachanov slowly came to life and levelled the score in the fourth set with two dominant tie-breakers.

With the fifth set also pushed into a tie-break, Kyrgios used his skill and feather-touch to push the Russian back with a fast serve before gently tapping the ball over the net to take a 3-0 lead in the final tie-break.

Khachanov wasn't done, though; the Russian sensed it was his time and brought the scores back to take the lead 4-3 with some breathtaking shot play.

As both competitors stood on weary legs at 7-7, it was Kyrgios who surged forward to win it 10-8 and seal the match. Kyrgios had managed to turn a potentially dominant win into a possible loss, then climb off the canvas, and ignore his ailing hip and hand for a last-gasp triumph.

This was a rollercoaster match for the ages.

2014 WIMBLEDON 4R vs. RAFAEL NADAL
7-6 (7-5), 5-7, 7-6 (7-5), 6-3.

This was the match that announced Nick Kyrgios to the world.

This victory was – and probably still is – the greatest of his career and one of the most significant victories in tennis history.

There may have been better finals matches. The Bjorn Borg v John McEnroe Wimbledon Final of 1980 is universally regarded as the greatest. Yet there is something about Kyrgios's fourth-round victory over Nadal that makes it the quintessential David v Goliath story.

The nuts and bolts: Kyrgios was granted a wildcard entrance into the tournament, became the first male on debut to reach the Wimbledon quarter-finals since German Florian Mayer in 2004, and also became the first wildcard to make a major quarter-final since Croatian Goran Ivanisevic in 2001.

His victory over Nadal was the first time since 1992 that a player ranked outside the top 100 had beaten a World No. 1.

At 19 years and 65 days old, he was also the youngest male to defeat a World No. 1 since Nadal himself defeated Roger Federer in the 2005 French Open semi-finals on his 19th birthday, 3 June.

In the first round, Kyrgios defeated Frenchman Stephane Robert 7-6 (7-2), 7-6 (7-1), 6-7 (6-8), 6-2, finishing him off comfortably in the fourth set after dropping the third. In the second round, Kyrigos faced a difficult opponent in world No. 13 Richard Gasquet. He mounted a remarkable comeback after losing the first two sets, saving nine match points, finishing the three-hour and 53-minute match with 86 winners and 21 aces (a sign of things to come).

He won 3-6, 6-7 (4-7), 6-4, 7-5, 10-8.

Facing Czech Jiri Vesely in the third round, the pair were forced to wait four and a half hours due to constant rain, with Vesely up 4-2 (30-0) in the first set. Again, Kyrgios mounted a strong comeback winning the next three sets, including the fourth set comfortably - 3-6, 6-3, 7-5, 6-2.

Now facing the World No. 1 on centre-court at Wimbledon for the first time of his career, Kyrgios entered the court with his pink headphones and looked cool as a cucumber. He appeared unfazed by the occasion as he aced Nadal out wide to win the first set tie-break 7-5. The powerful Spaniard worked his way back into the second set, winning it 7-5. With another Nadal comeback looming (he lost the first set and won the game in the first round, second round, and third round of Wimbledon 2014), Kyrgios showed the crowd this wasn't going to be any regular fourth round match with one of the most outrageous tennis shots ever seen. He produced a "tweener" from behind the baseline. It was later called the shot of the year.

Nadal served wide to Kyrgios's backhand at 40-love, with the games locked at 3-3. Kyrgios's return landed deep at the Spaniard's feet and he drove his forehand straight at Kyrgios who played the ball between his legs with a deft dab across court. The ball popped over the net leaving Nadal incredulous behind the baseline. Kyrgios raised his arms in celebration even managing a goofy smile to the gasps and celebrations of the crowd. The commentators called the shot outrageous. The "tweener" became synonymous with Kyrgios as is the underhand serve which is universally hated by all his opponents.

Similar to the first set, the third was an arm-wrestle between Kyrgios and Nadal and yet another tie-break. At 2-2, Kyrgios looked to have lost his cool after misjudging a double-handed backhand, and Nadal took the lead 5-4 before Kyrgios mounted a comeback, making Nadal spread wide and winning the tie-break 7-5, thanks to two Nadal errors.

Serving first in the fourth set, Nadal pushed himself back into the game leading 30-0, before Kyrgios displayed his serving prowess with three aces and took the early lead. The 19-year-old again pushed Nadal's serves wide and broke the world No. 1 for the first time. Showing maturity beyond his years, Kyrgios served out the match, winning the final set 6-3 and finishing the game with 37 aces to Nadal's 11.

2022 US Open 4R vs. Daniil Medvedev
7-6 (13-11), 3-6, 6-3, 6-2.

"A focused Nick Kyrgios is the most dangerous tennis player in the world." American Sportscaster Steve Wiessman summed it up beautifully after Kyrgios became the first player in 35 years to defeat a World No. 1 twice in the same year.

The last player to achieve this feat was fellow Australian Pat Rafter, who defeated American World No. 1, Ivan Lendl in 1987.

This victory was the greatest of Kyrgios's career so far, and one of the most significant victories in Australian Tennis history.

In front of a packed house at Arthur Ashe Stadium in New York City, Kyrgios wowed the big apple crowd disintegrating World No. 1 Daniil Medvedev in the third and fourth sets, moving into the quarter-finals for the first time at Flushing Meadows.

The clashes between Medvedev and Krygios are always scintillating, with this first set tie-breaker lasting more than an hour with Kyrgios surviving three set points, winning it 13-11. During the tie-break, Kyrgios directed his fury toward chair umpire Eva Asderaki-Moore berating her for starting the serve clock too early.

Inside the stadium, the humidity levels were high, and the air itself caused a build-up of tension as the two combatants created their very own storm on the court.

Again, Kyrgios looked ready to blow a fuse in the second set, coming within an inch of being evicted from the court after nearly hitting an errant ball into the stands toward spectators.

His newfound concentration levels were tested in the second set, with Medvedev powering to a 5-1 lead, eventually winning the set, 6-3.

Kyrigos yelled at his bench, asking them in no uncertain terms where he should "f***ing serve", It looked as though Medvedev had worked over Nick until he produced one of the strangest shots in Tennis history, leaving the spectators and commentators and the Tennis world in general baffled.

Kyrgios lost a point by oddly running around the net and hitting a ball from Medvedev that was clearly not going to make it over the net. Believing the shot was legal, Kyrgios celebrated the strange winner until Asderaki-Moore awarded the point to Medvedev, and Kyrgios had lost a break-point.

"I still can't believe the boneheaded play I made over here. I thought that was legal!", Kyrgios said after the game while talking to Patrick McEnroe on the court.

Sensing this would lead to another infamous Kyrgios's combustion, he rose to a superhuman level. He broke Medvedev on his next serve before powering to a 6-3 lead and taking a two-sets-to-one advantage.

A relentless erosion of Medvedev followed, with Kyrgios's strength and power too much, as he finished the last set 6-2 to claim an emphatic victory.

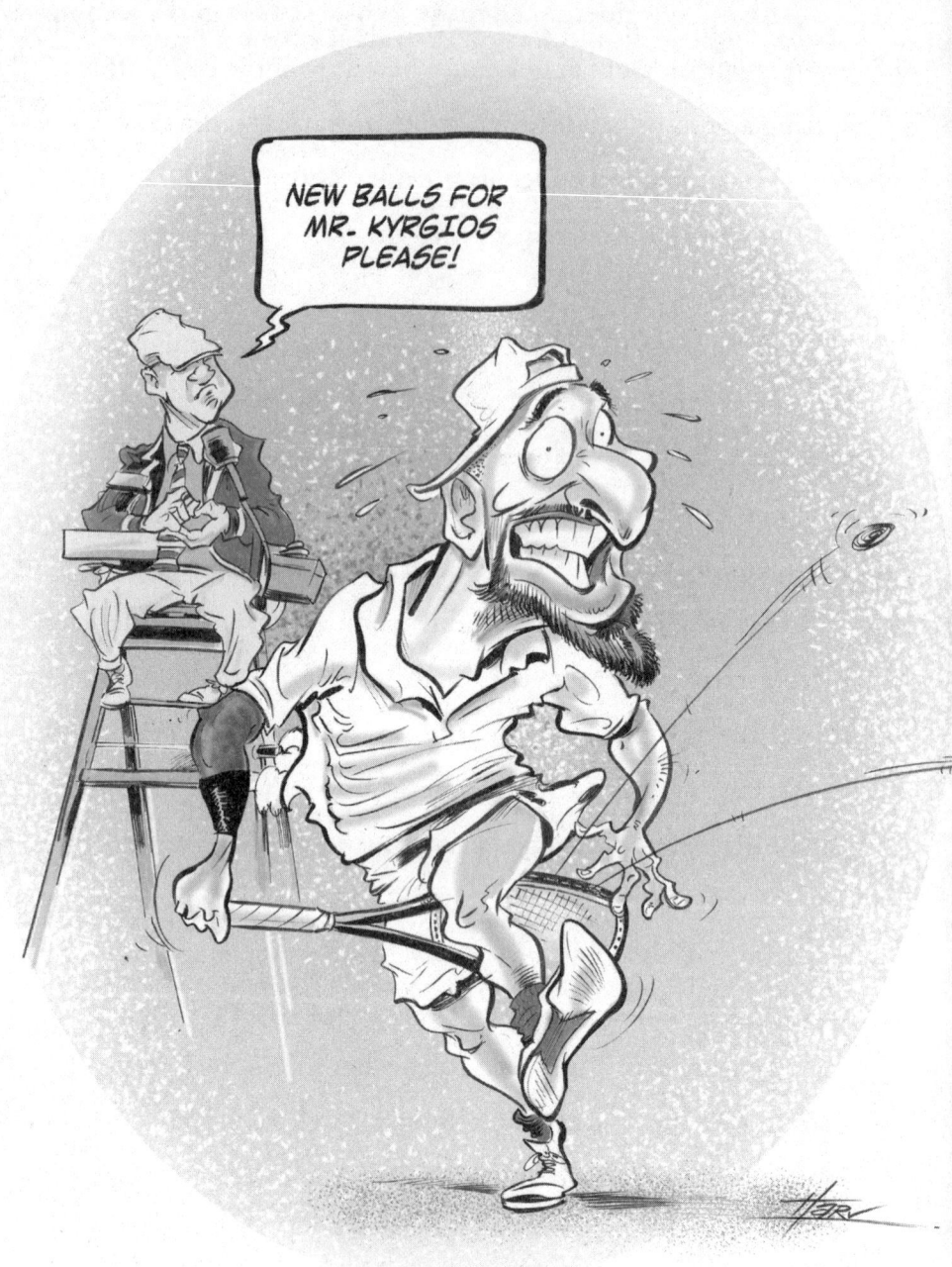

SHOT AT GLORY IN NEW YORK

" *I always wanted to win. I always felt like if I did the right things and played the right way, I could go deep. But obviously we all, my team and myself, had an eye on going home. We've been on the road for so long. That's how I am treating it. Had I lost tonight, a bit of doubles tomorrow, whatever happens, then we'd go home.*"
– Nick Kyrgios on his tilt at the US Open 2022.

The northern hemisphere summer of 2022 saw Nick Kyrgios emerge as a serious contender for a breakthrough Grand Slam championship, nine years after he began his pro career.

Until 2022 his best results in singles were quarter-final appearances in 2014 at Wimbledon and the 2015 Australian Open.

But in just two months – July and August – he was runner up to Serb Novak Djokovic in the Wimbledon final, took down World No. 1 Daniil Medvedev twice, including knocking him out of the US Open, and was considered a serious challenger for the US Open title after reaching the quarter-finals, the top two seeds already having been vanquished.

What was different?

Kyrgios explained he had changed his attitude: "I was very selfish. I felt like, I feel bad, I don't want to play. Then I looked at the people closest to me and how much I was letting them down, and I didn't want to do that anymore," he said in New York.

"I just tried to just look at my career. I was like, I feel like I've got so much left to give to the sport. That's it. I just trained hard. I just put my head down. Look, let's get in shape, better shape, first of all. Let's see, like, how it goes.

"Obviously winning helps. The motivation has been there. It's easy to train. It's easier to wake up obviously when things are going great.

"I was just really sick of letting people down. I feel like I'm making people proud now. I feel like there's not as much negative things being said about me. I just wanted to turn the narrative around almost. That's basically it. I just was feeling so depressed all the time, so feeling sorry for myself. I just wanted to change that."

Wimbledon was a turning point that saw him take on the US Open at Flushing Meadows with an open mind; if he was successful, he would be happy. If he lost early, he'd still be happy as that meant he could go home to Australia, where his parents were in ill-health.

His return home looked like being delayed somewhat when his victory over Daniil Medvedev and the loss by 2014 US Open champion Marin Cilic to Carlos Alcaraz meant there was no past Slam winner left in the US open draw.

He reached the quarter-finals for the first time. Did the No. 23 seed dare to dream?

It took No. 27 seed Russian Karen Khachanov three hours and 39 minutes over five tough sets to end the Kyrgios dream of a first Grand Slam in a match that began on the Tuesday night and finished on the Wednesday morning.

Khachanov won 7-5, 4-6, 7-5, 6-7 (3-7), 6-4 .

Kyrgios seemed to lack his usual energy. After a slow start, he battled hard to keep in touch with the Russian. The epic victory over top-seed Medvedev two nights previously had to have taken a toll on Kyrgios, and his knee appeared to give him trouble again although he said later he wasn't too bothered by it.

After dropping his serve to lose the first set, Kyrgios took a medical time-out, telling the trainer he felt a sharp pain in his left upper calf muscle.

He resumed but appeared to lack enthusiasm at the start of the second set. Something clicked though and he broke the Russian in the third game and held on to take the set.

There was life after all, and he had the crowd willing him on.

He dropped serve again to lose the third set but hope of a comeback was rekindled yet again when he grabbed the fourth set in a tie-breaker to force a decider. His record in matches that went to five sets was 11-3, so his fans were optimistic.

But there was to be no success this time.

He dropped serve in the first game of the decider and never recovered. But it was his career best performance at Flushing Meadows, despite the disappointing end to his run.

The telling statistic was the 58 unforced errors of Kyrgios, compared to Khachanov's 31. His break-point conversion rate was a low 22%. He won only two of the nine break-points he held.

Kyrgios obviously was devastated by the loss, despite all that he'd said previously about tennis, including his dislike for the game.

After shaking hands with Khachanov he smashed two

racquets on the court and walked off without changing his shoes or acknowledging the crowd.

Many tennis fans were not impressed and expressed their distaste on social media. But others defended him, saying the outburst showed how badly he wanted to win after his desire had been questioned in the past.

The 26-year-old Khachanov, a former world No. 8, fired 30 aces and hit 62 winners as he matched the power so often seen from Kyrgios, to reach his maiden semi-final of a Slam.

Asked afterwards if he'd play again in 2022, Kyrgios said: "Honestly I don't even really care about any other tournament. Like, I feel like at the Grand Slams, now having success at a Grand Slam, it's just like no other tournament really matters.

"It's like you get better, you get worse, and at a Grand Slam none of it matters. You either win or lose.

"People don't care if you got better on the day, or you lost (in) four (or) in the fifth, or you played one of the best matches of the tournament – you lost.

"That's all people remember at a Grand Slam, whether you win or you lose.

"I think pretty much every other tournament during the year is a waste of time. You just front up, show up at a Grand Slam. It's what you're remembered by.

"These four tournaments are the only ones that are ever going to matter. And it's just like you've got to start it all again, and I have to wait to the Australian Open.

"It's just devastating. It's heartbreaking. Not just for me but for everyone I know who wants me to win.

"But all credit to Karen. He's a fighter. He's a warrior. I thought he served really good today. Probably the best server I played this tournament, to be honest, the way he was hitting his spots under pressure."

It was the second time Kyrgios and Khachanov had played a five-setter at a Slam, with Kyrgios a third-round winner at the 2020 Australian Open in a match that went four-and-a-half hours with four tie-breaks.

"That's the only way to beat Nick, I think," Khachanov said after getting his revenge at Flushing Meadows two years later.

There were some Kyrgios moments. At the end of the first set he complained to his box: "I don't want to play through this shit. I really don't want to f***king do it."

Then he screamed at his box for lack of support: "You don't even know what a break-point is. An embarrassment."

He got a code violation for slamming his racquet down in disgust after failing to capitalise on break points and got another warning, for unsportsmanlike conduct, after throwing a water bottle on to the court. To finish, he smashed his racquets. Fines awaited him after the match. Thus ended the histrionics, and his tenure at the 2022 US Open.

For a change, one of the weirdest incidents during a Kyrgios match didn't involve him – two spectators were ejected after one gave the other a haircut in the stands.

FOOTNOTE: Another Australian and one-time Kyrgios girlfriend Ajla Tomljanovic also bowed out in the quarter-finals at Flushing Meadows. She lost to Tunisian Ons Jabeur in straight sets, although it was close, 6-4, 7-6 (7-4).

Tomljanovic had equalled her career-best Grand Slam finish after also making the quarter-finals at Wimbledon earlier in the year.

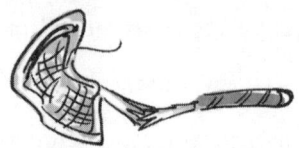

The Kyrgios-Medvedev round-of-16 match that preceded the quarter-final had pretty much the full Kyrgios package, from the brilliant to the baffling, as one commentator put it, as he triumphed over the World No. 1 in four sets, 7-6 (13-11), 3-6, 6-3, 6-2.

From the moment he baffled onlookers by gifting Medvedev a point that he would have won had he let the ball bounce instead of hitting it, Kyrgios seemed to spark into his best form.

He went on a big-hitting blitz, crushing balls on serve and hitting groundstroke winners at will.

He conceded the point that he gifted Medvedev with the score locked at 30-all on the Russian's serve was a "boneheaded" moment.

Kyrgios forced Medvedev into a skied shot that was not going to come back into his half of the court. But Kyrgios got between the net and the chair umpire to slam home what he thought was the winner.

He was pumped by his effort but was reminded by the chair

umpire that he had committed a foul shot after crossing the net and playing the ball in Medvedev's half of the court. That cost him a break-point and Medvedev eventually held serve.

Asked about it after the match Kyrgios said: "I still can't believe it. I still can't believe the bone-headed play I made over here," he said. "I thought that was legal. I'm gonna look like an idiot."

Nevertheless, victory eventually was his – another milestone in what proved to be his best season by far.

He'd won more matches on tour since the French Open than any other player, including victories over Stefanos Tsitsipas, Reilly Opelka, Frances Tiafoe, Tommy Paul and Medvedev.

As everyone has come to expect from a Kyrgios match, there were some tense moments.

At 5-5 in the marathon first set Kyrgios took exception to being warned over his pace of play by the chair umpire after he towelled himself down in the high humidity.

"I come back to the box and there is six seconds left. I've never had a problem with it this tournament apart from you," Kyrgios shouted at the umpire.

He then went back to his player box and said: "I'm dripping in sweat. I'm not supposed to wipe my hands?"

The confrontation continued at the change of ends with Kyrgios again questioning why he was being put under pressure.

"I've not had one issue. Not one in three months," he said.

"I play the fastest on tour. I'm getting back to the baseline with four seconds. What are you doing?"

In the first set that went to a long tie-breaker, he yelled at his box several times: "Tell me where to f****** serve."

In the second set, the crowd booed when Kyrgios smashed a ball into a barrier and had Medvedev asking the umpire if it was OK for him to do that too.

The fourth set saw Kyrgios earn a code violation for some bad language.

But he remained a crowd-pleaser: He waved his arms upwards towards the full-house at Arthur Ashe Stadium on break-point and the crowd responded with the noise that might be heard at the end of a match. Medvedev tried to get the crowd cheering for him. It wasn't quite "crickets", but he got nothing like the response given to Kyrgios.

Kyrgios wasn't impressed with Medvedev's attempts to woo the crowd and he responded by smashing three serves that got him out of trouble, each serve accompanied by a huge scream.

Vintage Kyrgios.

He got the upper hand in the third set and didn't look back.

Medvedev said later he started to feel worse physically late in the match, something he blamed on an illness that he believes was caused by excessive air conditioning.

"He played good," Medvedev said.

"It was really even til the third set. I started to feel worse physically.

"I felt sick today. I get sick at least once a year during the USA swing 'cause the air conditioning here is just crazy. Last year it was in Cincinnati, this year here."

The Russian pointed to one incident he wasn't happy about during the match. Ironically, the call that upset him came from Kyrgios's support bench that the Australian had regularly berated for not showing enough support.

At 5-6 down in the first set Medvedev had missed his first serve and was about to hit his second serve when he said he heard someone from the Kyrgios support seats call out "C'mon get him." Medvedev spoke to the umpire and Kyrgios after the match.

When asked about the incident in his post-match press conference Medvedev said: "It was 6-5 for him, first set, 40-30 on my serve. Just before the second serve somebody from his box was, 'C'mon, get him'.

"That's not nice. You shouldn't do it when you're in the other's box before the second serve. I told this to the umpire. I don't know who exactly it was. People who I see from him, actually must be honest, I don't know their names, but we just talked in the locker room. So I respect them like probably I respect almost every other team.

"But at the end of the match, I was like, 'C'mon, he shouldn't do it'. It was a man's voice. It was only once, so probably also it was not like on purpose – I hope. So that's fine."

The loss guaranteed the 26-year-old Medvedev would lose his world No. 1 ranking at the end of the tournament.

For Kyrgios, he was in the quarter-finals for the first time.

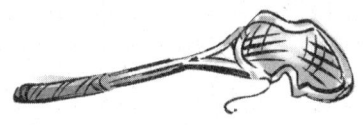

Nick Kyrgios faced challenges on and off the court, including a different kind of court altogether, as he prepared to finish his campaign in the US in the latter part of 2022.

The incident at Wimbledon when he accused a fan of being drunk came to haunt him when the fan revealed she was suing the Australian for defamation over his remarks.

The plaintiff, Anna Palus, a Polish lawyer, said: "Not only did this cause considerable harm on the day, resulting in my temporary removal from the arena, but Mr Kyrgios's false allegation was broadcast to, and read by, millions around the world, causing me and my family very substantial damage and distress.

"I am not litigious, but after much consideration, I have concluded that I have no alternative but to instruct my solicitors Brett Wilson LLP to bring defamation proceedings against Mr Kyrgios in order to clear my name. The need to obtain vindication, and to prevent repetition of the allegation, are the only reasons for taking legal action."

Kyrgios already had a court date back in Canberra, Australia, arising from his split from a former girlfriend.

None of that seemed to weigh too heavily on him as he began his assault on the US Open men's singles title; hearing dates were still well into the future.

He would have been more interested in what lay ahead in terms of tennis opponents. His seeding gave him a reasonable run in the first three rounds. It would get tougher after that, including a likely date with World No. 1 and defending champion Daniil

Medvedev. At least, Kyrgios knew he could beat the Russian, having done so just a few weeks earlier in Montreal. Just getting to the fourth round for that clash was Kyrgios's best effort in the US Open; he'd never before made it past the third round.

Former World No. 1 and US Open No. 2 seed Raphael Nadal was another possible obstacle if Kyrgios was to have a shot at his first Grand Slam. American Frances Tiafoe, beaten by Kyrgios in the quarter-finals at the Citi Open in Washington a month earlier, took care of that by ousting the Spaniard in four sets in the round of 16 and ending Nadal's 22-match winning streak.

All eyes were on Kyrgios even before his stunning progress towards a shot at glory for which he was considered a 15.1% chance, third behind No.2 Rafael Nadal (16.7 per cent) and No.3 Carlos Alcaraz (23.1 per cent). Nadal's demise increased his prospects considerably as did his win over Medvedev and some commentators even considered him the favourite to win the title.

For starters, he had a good record on hard courts. Of his 11 tour-level finals, nine were on that surface, as were all seven of his championships – Marseille 2016, Atlanta 2016, Tokyo 2016, Brisbane 2018, Acapulco 2019 and Washington 2019 and 2022.

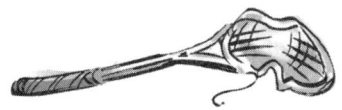

The US Open organisers didn't miss a chance to put on a crowd-pleaser in the first round, scheduling Nick Kyrgios's match against fellow Australian Thanasi Kokkinakis in a prime spot – last match on Arthur Ashe court on opening night.

The honour of that would usually be reserved for the defending champion or World No. 1, even a hometown hero.

The decision recognised the star quality of the Australian, both in the US and world-wide. It would be cynical to suspect they were hoping for fireworks, a little less likely against his good mate.

Kyrgios was relaxed about his prospects, even saying he wasn't worried about losing early as that would mean he could get home to his ailing parents sooner.

He'd also been doing some tourist things. His mother had told of her concerns that Kyrgios had been reluctant to step outside his "bubble" and take in the sites and experiences of tennis venues while he was on tour.

That seemed to change around Wimbledon and getting out and about was on his agenda in the US.

He and girlfriend Costeen Hatzi posed for a photos atop the Empire State Building, visiting Times Square and at Central Park Zoo, and according to one report they attended a Broadway show.

Then it was down to business at Flushing Meadows.

The match between the Special Ks (who would later contest the doubles) was to follow another crowd-pleaser, Serena Williams playing her last Grand Slam tournament before retirement.

Her first-round match against Danka Kovinic was her 1012th in a 27-year career in which she'd won 23 Grand Slams.

Kyrgios paid tribute to Williams. "It's obviously a very special moment for her. She's probably the greatest of all-time," he said.

"Whether or not we see anyone deliver the career that she has, I don't think that's possible.

"I'll just kind of chill out, follow the score to see what my warm-up is and all that, but that's for her. I don't know the amount of emotion she's dealing with. I couldn't imagine it.

"It would be so exhausting. Everyone's talking about it, everybody wanting to know how she feels.

"I just want her to enjoy the moment. I'm sure she'll have a lot of nostalgic feelings out there. Hopefully, she wins. I wouldn't want to see her lose.

"It would be a pretty cool story if she went out with a great result."

Williams defeated Kovinic 6-3, 6-2 to continue towards what she hoped could be a glorious ending to her career. She defeated second seed Anett Kontaveit 7-6, 2-6, 6-2, in the second round and faced World No. 46 Australian Ajla Tomljanovic (a former girlfriend of Kyrgios) in the third round.

Tomljanovic spoiled the Serena farewell party, ousting her in three sets, 7-5, 6-7, 6-1 and thus denying her the chance to Match Australian Margaret Court's 24 singles titles. Williams was at pains to avoid using the word "retirement," saying she found it an outdated term, but the end to her stellar career was imminent and the fans hailed her as if it was the last time they would see her at Flushing Meadows.

Kyrgios got off to a good start, too.

He took just 30 minutes to claim the first set 6-3 against his doubles partner. The match tightened up after that but Kyrgios prevailed in three sets, 6-3, 6-4 and 7-6 (tie break), joining five other Australian first-round winners in the men's singles. Only Kyrgios and De Minaur (seeded 18) survived the second round.

Kyrgios said after defeating Kokkinakis for his 200th ATP Tour win: "That was the most uncomfortable I've ever felt on a tennis court.

"I was really trying to not look at him at all, and I felt like that kind of helped me."

"It was really uncomfortable. I don't want to do that again, to be honest."

There was customary yelling at his player's box. Three sets into the Kokkinakis clash, Kyrgios took aim at those in his box who, in his opinion, were not making enough noise or standing up on his points.

"Stand up on my points," he yelled.

"It's legal now, IT'S LEGAL," a reference to the fact a player's a box could coach during the match for the first time at a Slam.

The biggest surprise on Day One was the demise of No. 4 seed Stefanos Tsitsipas in four sets at the hands of world No. 94 and qualifier Colombian Daniel Elahi Galan.

When Kyrgios came up against World No. 50, Benjamin Bonzi, of France, in the second round there was an entirely new ground for complaint.

Midway through the second set, Kyrgios said he could smell marijuana smoke from the stands. He continued to complain during a change of ends, asking that a warning be given to the crowd.

The umpire first thought Kyrgios was referring to smoke from food. "You don't even want to remind anyone not to do it?", Kyrgios said. "It was f***ing marijuana. Obviously I'm not going to be complaining about food stuff. Obviously not.

"Obviously when athletes are running side-to-side and they have asthma already it's probably not ideal."

An ESPN reporter confirmed the smell of marijuana.

A warning was then issued to the crowd as the two players returned to the court. "Ladies and gentlemen, a reminder that you cannot smoke on court," the umpire cautioned. (Recreational cannabis is legal in the state of New York, but the US Open does not permit any kind of smoking).

Kyrgios outlined his asthma issues in his post-match press conference.

"People don't know but I'm a heavily asthmatic so when I'm running side to side and I'm struggling to breathe already, it's not something I want to be breathing in in between points," he said.

There was another dramatic piece during the match. Kyrgios was issued a code violation warning for unsportsmanlike behaviour after he swore towards his player's box and spat on the court in the third set.

Kyrgios lost the set but recovered to win the match 7-6 (3), 6-4, 4-6 and 6-4.

He drew a wild-card entrant in the third round, American Jeff Wolf who had only been a pro for a year and had beaten No.

16 seed Roberto Bautista Agut in the second round. Wolf was no match for Kyrgios, falling in straight sets in just under two hours.

Kyrgios won 6-4, 6-2, 6-3, with a minimum of yelling at his box and a touch of comedy when he showed off a few of his dance moves.

He said afterwards: "It was a very tough match for me. I knew J.J. is home crowd favourite. I knew I had to be on my guns today and serve well. I'm just really happy to move forward."

Kyrgios fired 21 aces in improving his 2022 win-loss record to 34-9 (13-2 since the Wimbledon final).

The "Special Ks" won their first-round US Open doubles against Hugo Gaston of France and Lorenzo Musetti of Italy. It was a much closer game than world doubles rankings suggested. Kyrgios (18) and Kokkinakis (22) should have been far too strong for Gaston (227) and Musetti (304) but were challenged all the way, dropping the first set 4-6 before recovering to take the next two 6-3 and 6-4.

They advanced to the round of 16 with a straight sets win over Yoshihito Nishioka (Japan) and Andre Goransson (Sweden), 6-4, 7-6. That was as far as they got, losing in three sets after winning the first in the round of 16 to similarly-ranked Harri Heliovarra (Finland) and Lloyd Glasspool (Great Britain). Disappointing, but it left Kyrgios free to focus on his singles campaign.

The round of 16 in doubles also saw another Australian pair, Matt Ebden and Matt Purcell bow out, leaving Kyrgios and

Tomljanovic as the country's hopes for US Open glory. Both came up short, but earned accolades for what they brought to the tournament.

De Minaur bowed out of the singles in the round of 32, beaten in four sets by Spaniard Pablo Carrena Busta who in turn was beaten in the round of 16 in a tough five-setter by Russian Karen Khachanov, Kyrgios's quarter-final opponent.

FOOTNOTE: The news from the 2022 US Open wasn't all bad for Australia. John Peers and Storm Sanders won the mixed doubles title — the first Aussie pair in 21 years to do so, and the first Australians to win a mixed doubles grand slam title since at the 2013 Australian Open.

Other US Open championship winners: Men's singles – 19-year-old Spaniard Carlos Alcaraz (new World No. 1 and the youngest male to be so). Women's singles – Iga Swiatek (Poland); Women's doubles – Barbora Krejcikova (Czech) and Katerina Siniakova (Czech). Men's Doubles – Rajeev Ram (US) and Joe Salisbury (UK).

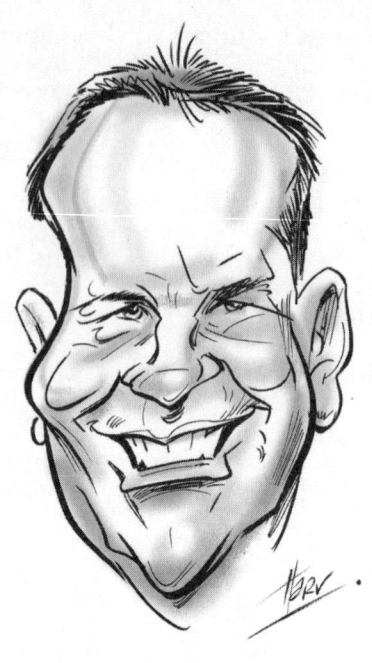

The Poms, they just couldn't get enough of him. I think they were disappointed on the occasions when he just went out and played tennis and didn't have any tantrums, didn't have any sort of, you know, blow-ups or anything like that.

TONY JONES

SWINGING THROUGH NORTH AMERICA

Nick Kyrgios hadn't been in a singles final for three years but in 2022 he made it two-in-a-row inside a month.

His rise in rankings would be significant going to Flushing Meadows for the US Open as a seeding there would mean he'd be most unlikely to draw a Top 10 player in the early rounds.

Some big names were missing from the entry list and some others faced challenges to be able to give it their best shot.

Roger Federer led the list of absentees form North America, the former citing a foot injury that saw him play just twice since the French Open. Raphael Nadal was also a doubtful starter, at least until the US Open. He hadn't played since conceding an injury walkover to Kyrgios at Wimbledon.

Dominic Thiem, US Open champion in 2020. was also absent, suffering a wrist injury over the summer from which he hadn't recovered.

One more withdrawal was to come.

For Kyrgios's conqueror at Wimbledon, Novak Djokovic, there was to be no American swing, including the US Open.

His failure to be vaccinated against Covid meant he was not eligible to enter the US, just as was the case for the Australian Open earlier in the year when he was sent home without firing a shot.

There was an outcry, former US great John McEnroe leading the charge to have the Wimbledon champion excluded from the country's point-of-entry rules. Petitions were started and the Government even said it was considering proposals to ease the entry rules. But there was no reprieve.

There were other question marks.

Russian Daniil Medvedev had played only one tournament since June after the Wimbledon ban. Lack of tournament play would be a significant drawback.

The same circumstances applied to countryman Andrey Rublev, although he tuned up at Washington by reaching the semi-finals, seeded No. 1, only to bow out to Yoshihito Nishioka.

German Alexander Zverev hadn't played competition since the French Open where he retired with a serious ankle injury. It was doubtful whether he would play in the US before the Open.

Against the background of all that, several pundits thought Kyrgios would be capable of really good results in the US, provided he remained injury-free.

When the seedings for the US Open came out after Djokovic's withdrawal, Kyrgios was 23 of 32, meaning he would not necessarily have to face another seeded player until deep in the tournament if he lasted long enough. He was disappointed to learn he'd face good mate and doubles partner Thanasi Kokkinakis in the first round. His draw also put him in the same grouping as Medvedev.

Reaching the final at Wimbledon was Kyrgios's major achievement in terms of on-court success.

Though beaten in the final, Wimbledon wasn't the end of his

stellar season. His four sets loss to Novak Djokovic was his only loss in 11 matches since the middle of June as he moved on to the North American hardcourt swing.

The swing schedule included Atlanta, Washington, Cincinnati, Montreal, and Winston-Salem before Flushing Meadows. He wasn't going to play them all. Washington was a certainty as he'd won there at his previous appearance, in 2019. He was given a wildcard entry for Cincinnati and by the time he finished at Washington his name was down for a first-round match in Montreal for the Canadian Open. He was going to miss Winston-Salem.

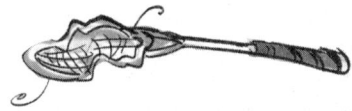

First stop on the 2022 North American hardcourt swing at the beginning of August 2022 was Atlanta as Kyrgios set himself for a tilt at the US Open in New York at the end of the month and into September.

There was an injury concern right away – he pulled out of the singles in Atlanta with knee soreness but persevered with doubles where he and Thanasi Kokkinakis collected the silverware to add to the title they won in Melbourne at the Australian Open at the start of the year.

Kyrgios went into the Atlanta Open as the seventh seed and was drawn to play German Peter Gojowczyk in the round of 32. But he appeared before the crowd just before the match was to begin to say he was pulling out as his knee was bothering him.

"First of all, I just want to say I'm extremely shattered that I'm not able to compete tonight," Kyrgios said as he revealed his withdrawal.

"I've won this tournament once and I've played probably some of the best tennis of my career. All I wanted to do was come out here and give you guys a show, obviously just see what I'm capable of.

"But I'm unable to give out my best performance today and I'm just extremely sorry. But I'm going to keep my hopes up and maybe be able to continue doubles with Thanasi (Kokkinakis) this week.

"I hope you all won't be too hard on me; I was going to come out here and see you guys face-to-face to tell you that I love you guys and hopefully next year in singles I'll be able to compete and give it my all."

He was able to continue in the doubles with fellow Australian Kokkinakis, the Special Ks as they were dubbed in Australia, taking out the final against fellow Australians Jason Kubler and John Peers, 7-6 (7-4), 7-5.

Kyrgios and Kokkinakis, who won the Australian Open men's doubles in January 2022, entered the tournament as the No. 2 seeds. They intended to join again for the US Open doubles.

Withdrawal from the Atlanta singles meant Kyrgios dropped out of the top 60 of the ATP rankings, to 63, and faced the prospect of going into the US Open unseeded and facing a difficult draw. The ship was righted in Washington.

Despite Kyrgios's withdrawal, the Atlanta singles was still a triumph for Australia; Alex De Minaur defeated American Jenson Brooksby 6-3, 6-3, repeating his title win of three years before. It was the 23-year-old's first victory since June 2021 in Eastbourne and his sixth ATP Tour title overall. His victories were at the Sydney International 2019, Atlanta Open 2019, Zhuhai Championships 2019, Antalya Open 2021, Eastbourne International 2021 and the Atlanta Open 2022

De Minaur, too, was using the US hardcourt swing to prepare for a shot at the US Open. He made the round of 16 at Wimbledon earlier in July and was third seed in Atlanta. His ranking moved up to No. 21, then to 20 after Washington, improving his chances of a good draw at Flushing Meadows in the year's last "major" for which he was seeded 19.

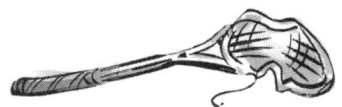

In Washington a week after Atlanta, Kyrgios became the first person to win the Citi Open men's singles and doubles (with American Jack Sock) titles at the same tournament and the first Australian to win the singles title more than once.

His seventh ATP career title produced his fifth semi-final appearance in his seven most recent tournaments. He said: "I feel like I have really kind of reinvented myself this year."

His repeat win (the first was in 2019) in Washington gave

him a 7-4 winning career record in finals.

He was asked: "Is it too much to say your success at Wimbledon reignited something in you? How would you explain, if anything, what it did to you inside, commitment wise?"

He gave a measured answer: "I feel like I have been feeling like this for the last, I'd say, almost eight months. Before Oz Open I decided that I really wanted to put in a good training block, and then things just started falling into place.

"The rest of my life started, just everything was really good. You know, I had a great Australian Open. I felt like the tournaments after Australian Open I was kind of reinventing myself a little bit on the court. I was incredibly intense, playing some really good matches, had some great results earlier in the year.

"Played a great grass court season. Made a couple semi-finals and was right there. I was always knocking on the door of a singles title. I was waiting for it. I felt like I was, you know, one of the best players in the world this year by far.

"I feel if I had points from Wimbledon, I'd be nearing on the top 10. So, you know, I feel like I have really kind of reinvented myself this year." (ranking points were not awarded at Wimbledon in 2022 as Russian and Belarus players were excluded).

How was his focus and motivation? "I feel as if I'm a lot older, a lot more mature, and I feel like when you play on the tour and you age and you get older, you realise you shouldn't be taking these things for granted, the way you're feeling, the way your body feels.

"Also, I have a partner with me now I see a future with,

and I kind of see that I have to provide for (us). So I feel like my motivation is a lot higher than it used to be.

"I just feel like there is a small window I should capitalise on it. I don't care about what people say about my tennis, like always disrespectful to the sport, all this, all that. I know that deep down that I try really hard to do it my own way. I know that I inspire millions of people, and I'm just playing for them.

"You know, I wouldn't even say I'm playing for myself at this point. I just want to go out there, have fun, try my best, and do it my way. I think that people are starting to see that a little bit more."

Kyrgios had eased through the Citi Open holding serve 64 times without being broken, defeating the World No. 96, Japan's Nishioka 6-4, 6-3 in the final in just on 80 minutes. There was just one code violation – no fines – and even some moments of humour.

"This is amazing," Kyrgios said in his post-match, on-court interview. "It is emotional for me to be back here again and claim another title."

He took a little time to compose himself after the final point.

"It was emotional for me to see where I was last year to now, it's an incredible transformation," Kyrgios said. "I just came out with great energy because I knew I had the experience on my side today.

"I love this court, I played so many good matches here. I'm just really happy with myself.

"I've been in some really dark places and just to be able to turn it around...

"There's so many people who have helped me get there but

myself, I've shown some serious strength to just continue and just persevere and get through those really tough times and still be able to perform in tournaments like this one."

The best player he came up against in Washington was fourth seed American Reilly Opleka. Nishioka may have done Kyrgios a favour by taking out top-seed and world No. 8 Russian Andrey Rublev in the semi-finals while he had to contend with the World No. 115, Swede Mikael Ymer.

Kyrgios might have been drained physically, even mentally, but he backed up straight after his singles win to take the doubles title with American Jack Sock.

They defeated defeat Ivan Dodig and Austin Krajicek 7-5. 6-4, to give Kyrgios his third doubles title for the year.

Kyrgios's fitness, as it turned out, was severely tested. When bad weather intervened, he had to play his quarter-final and semi-final on the same day. He also faced the prospect of backing up for the doubles with American Jack Sock. Fortunately, the doubles semi-final didn't go ahead on the same day of the singles as their opponents conceded a walkover.

While that put Kyrgios and Sock into the final, they were going to have to play within an hour of the last point in the singles final.

Kyrgios conceded he had to have some treatment after his energy-sapping workload when he defeated American Reilly Opelka, then saved five match points in an epic quarter-final win over another American, Frances Tiafoe.

The match against Tiafoe was tough. After saving five match points, Kyrgios didn't wrap up his 6-7 (5), 7-6 (12), 6-2 victory until nearly 1 a.m. the next day.

Would he have enough left in the tank for his semi-final against Swede Mikael Ymer?

He did. He took an hour and 34 minutes to secure a spot in the final without facing a single break point.

Described in the *Washington Post* newspaper as a "maverick" Kyrgios's run in Washington was punctuated more by flamboyance than meltdowns.

As his quarter-final dragged on into the early hours of the next day, he yelled: "I want to go to bed" during the third set.

Kyrgios wasn't impressed with a delay in his first match, against Tommy Paul.

With Paul serving at 4-5 (30-40) in the second set, the umpire said there was a power loss in the stadium and delayed play briefly.

After Paul saved the match point with a forehand winner, Kyrgios was shaking his head. He then received a code violation for ball abuse, to which he responded by giving the umpire one of his own. He said: "What about a code violation for the bad idea by you to slow the game down?"

After his first-round victory over Paul he complained about being drug-tested at midnight.

"Last night, I played a first round, tough first round, and I got drug tested until 12 a.m. Midnight and (was) expected to play tonight." The Wimbledon runner-up also said he had been told to eat in the tournament cafe which left him feeling aggrieved.

"He (a seeded player) gets to bed at the time he wants to get to bed. Eats what he wants to eat. I was told to eat in the cafe when there was no food," he added. "These are just things I think a seeded player won't have to deal with."

There was more trouble ahead that would test his patience.

He wasn't happy that his third-round match was suspended just seven minutes into the first set due to rain and lightning. At 1-1 in the opening set, the chair umpire called a suspension of play and Kyrgios went to the bench, shrugged his shoulders and asked "Why?" No doubt the reasons were explained to him, as the weather was particularly bad (it was later reported lightning caused three deaths elsewhere in the Washington area).

A quibble over a shot-clock call didn't amount to anything much, perhaps surprising given his outbursts in previous tournaments.

In his first-round match he reintroduced a novelty from his 2019 Citi Open-winning run, asking a fan in the front row where to serve on match point. Kyrgios apologised and felt obliged to her after missing the target on his first serve, following up with a vicious second attempt that Marcos Giron couldn't return.

He also showed a more caring side in the match against Paul.

A woman sitting directly behind Paul was hit in the head when a return of serve from Kyrgios bounced over the wall at the back of the court.

The woman appeared shocked but otherwise unhurt. Kyrgios inquired about her from the other end of the court and later gave her one of the tournament's (clean) towels after switching ends and checking she was OK.

Kyrgios also had the crowd laughing when he thanked the umpires, saying: "The relationship is still rocky with the umpires, but I just want to say thank you to everyone."

He also thanked the "ball kids" before realising they weren't really kids, correcting himself to say, "the ball women and men too."

Overall, it was a much-restrained Nick Kyrgios performance, perhaps aware that turning on the tantrums would not endear him to the crowd as he faced four Americans in succession.

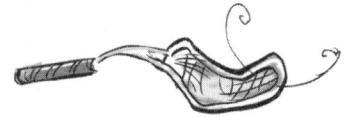

By the time Kyrgios reached the ATP 1000 at Montreal in August 2022, he had collected a singles and two doubles titles – and he hadn't had too much trouble with officialdom either.

The peace and quiet didn't last long.

Kyrgios was on a roll as he began his Canada Open tilt. The first round saw him triumph 6-4, 6-4 over world No. 32 Sebastian Baez.

A major upset was next. He faced World No. 1 Daniil Medvedev in the second round, unlucky to draw him so early but without a seeding he had to accept the cards he was dealt.

His victory was hard-fought over just on two hours – he

dropped the first set in a tie-break but rallied to take the next two, winning 6-7 (2), 6-4, 6-2.

He fired 12 aces against four double faults, and faced only two break points, saving both.

It was his second win over a reigning world No.1 for Kyrgios, but his first in eight years. In 2014, a teenage Kyrgios stunned then-No.1 Rafael Nadal to reach his first Grand Slam quarter-final, at Wimbledon.

His next match at Montreal pitted him against fellow-Australian Alex De Minaur. That produced yet another outburst at his box and support team. As De Minaur broke him late in the match, Kyrgios – as he had done before – blew up at his team for their "lack of support". This time, he quickly recovered.

"(Today was) incredibly tough," he said after defeating De Minaur. "After yesterday's big high, after playing Daniil and the crowd was amazing, it's a day I'll probably never forget.

"Today was really hard mentally for me to go out and play Alex, we're such good friends and he's been having such a good career so far and carrying the Australian flag for so long, it was tough mentally to play a friend, especially if they're Australian.

"I just got out here and got the job done. I played the way I had to play. He's a helluva player, if he plays to his strengths, he's one of the best players from the back of the court and he's so fast."

After Kyrgios disposed of world No. 1 Medvedev, American Andy Roddick, a former world No. 1 himself, said Kyrgios was "at par" with the Big 3 on physical ability.

"Just based on physical ability I think he's the only guy that can even compare to the Big 3 of this generation but I still don't know is it gonna explode," Roddick said. "He's played a lot of tennis. Is it just a time bomb?"

The comments turned out to be somewhat prophetic, Kyrgios complaining of stomach muscle problems after losing to Pole Hubert Hurkacz in the quarter-final.

The clash with Hurkacz also saw a flare-up when the Pole took a toilet break with Kyrgios left to swelter in the heat waiting for him to return. He later explained that he had stiffened up during the break.

At the time, he protested. "Why did he change clothes? I don't need. Nobody needs," he was heard saying to the umpire. "No-one needs to change f***** clothes in f***** 15-degree heat. 15 f***** degrees bro."

Hurkacz returned to go on and win 6-7 (4), 7-6 (5) 1-6.

After the match Kyrgios was less combative: "When you stop playing for five, 10 minutes, it doesn't help your body," he said. "My body was so stiff after that; I couldn't move properly. My abdominal was hurting. It's within the rules [toilet breaks], so I'm not going to complain. I just completely stiffened up."

Though Kyrgios failed to reach the semi-finals his progress was enough to put him inside the top 32 of world rankings and earn a seeding for the US Open in September.

His next aim was to get inside the top 16 seedings for Flushing Meadows and avoid higher ranked opponents at least until the second week. He could do that with a good run at the South Western Open in Cincinnati, Ohio.

In terms of his prospects of being competitive in the US Open a loss to Pole Hubert Hurkacz probably was no bad thing.

He had secured a seeding for the US Open and his body would have a little more time to recover before Cincinnati. "My body hasn't been feeling great the last week," he said.

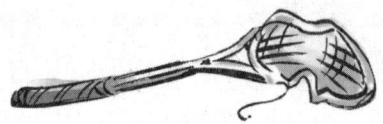

Getting a wildcard entry at Cincinnati in his last hit-out before the US Open was a good pick-up for Kyrgios He was runner-up in 2017, beating Rafael Nadal on the way to the final where he lost to Grigor Dimitrov.

There's something about the Cincinnati Masters (Southern and Western Open) tournament that seemed to bring out aggression in Nick Kyrgios.

It was there, in 2019, that he was fined $US 11,300 for a series of indiscretions.

He also believes he has played some of his best tennis there, even though he hadn't made it past the second round in singles in his past two visits.

"I have played some amazing tennis here in my career, and I have also had some crazy outbursts, as well," he said after winning his first-round match against Spaniard Alejandro Davidovich Fokina.

In 2019 he landed in hot (make that boiling) water over

on-court incidents. His meltdown that resulted in heavy fines included smashing racquets and spitting towards a referee.

In his second-round 7–6, 6–7, 2–6 loss to eighth seed Russian Karen Khachanov, Kyrgios's trouble started when he was given a time violation and made comments to the chair umpire, Ferguson Murphy, saying the whole thing was "hilarious, bro," and pointed to the chair saying, "absolute rubbish... disgrace." He was upset about the starting of the time clock began and thought he was playing just as quickly, if not faster, than other top players.

The Australian was vocal throughout the match, and in the third set called Murphy "the worst f***k-ing referee ever" after getting a violation code. He then headed into the tunnel for what was said to be a bathroom break, taking two rackets and a towel with him. His anger was obvious and he was seen to smash racquets in the tunnel.

He didn't get a violation for the racquet abuse but was given a time violation for the time taken to regrip his racquets. He appeared to spit in the direction of the umpire as he walked off at the end of the match.

That was 2019. Roll on to 2022 and Kyrgios was in trouble again, in his first-round match against Davidovich Fokina, the man who put Novak Djokovic out of the Masters on Monte Carlo earlier in 2022.

One of the incidents that earned him a code violation this time ironically was similar to that for which he called for Tsitsipas to be defaulted during their clash in Wimbledon a month earlier.

Kyrgios sent a ball flying into the stands out of frustration early in the second set and was given a code a code violation but was spared being defaulted. He regained his composure to win convincingly but earned the ire of the crowd which soundly booed him. He hit more balls into the grandstand.

He'd also yet again rounded on his player's box. How much longer his supporters could tolerate such behaviour was a fair question.

The upside for wild-card Kyrgios was his tennis; he produced 29 winners – including 10 aces – and three breaks of the Spaniard's serve to reach the second round with a 7-5, 6-4 victory.

The win gave Kyrgios a clean sheet of first-round victories in the season and his 22nd win since returning to the ATP Tour in June after skipping the clay season.He said after the match: "Physically, I didn't feel the best, but you have to keep pushing, keep trying."

He didn't make it past the second round, bundled out in just under an hour by rising American star Taylor Fritz.

Again there was controversy – he blew up at the umpire and was warned to stop using the F word. He was booed by the crowd which wasn't impressed with his effort (or apparent lack of it).

He seemed to be distracted by other goings on – he complained about "standards" while pointing out problems with the court surface, fans walking in and out between points and flickering on-court screens.

As it turned out, it seemed his troublesome knee had flared up again.

He always knew Fritz would be a difficult opponent. After the first round he said of Fritz who he was to face next: "It's an extremely tough matchup for me. Obviously not going to get much rhythm. You know, he's extremely confident. He's one of the players I think that never doubts himself. He backs himself. He believes that he's one of the best players in the world. That's what makes him so dangerous. He's had wins over Nadal."

Kyrgios departed the Cincinnati singles with a world ranking of 26, secure in the seedings for his next stop, the US Open in just under two weeks.

But how was his fitness?

Former World No. 4 Greg Rusedski, in commentary on Amazon Prime, cast fears over Kyrgios's ability to perform.

"It did unravel," Rusedski said. "You're worried about the knee physically. It's a lot easier to do on grass courts than hard courts.

"You can hear the boos around the stadium. They don't feel like he gave it his best effort out there and we're hoping the knee isn't too serious but he's got to show more. He's improved out of sight but physically he's got to get stronger."

At the press conference after his first-round win, Kyrgios shed some light on his emotions on the court. He was asked what had changed since 2019.

"I feel like I have just been an emotional kind of tennis player my entire career," he said. "Ever since I picked up a racquet, my mum used to watch me throw tantrums and cry on the court and be emotional when I lost.

"I think that's, in a way, just me showing that I do care about the result. I think that's important. You know, a kid should care about the result, and I have never really accepted losing, you know, without beating myself up after the match or during the match. You know, I have always cared about the results so much.

"But I definitely feel like, yeah, it's a part of me that if I went out on the court and I was so emotional on every point and cared too much, I think you'd definitely see me throw my racquet. You rarely see me throw my racquet anymore. You get the occasionally outburst, but no more than another player.

"I feel like that's something I've worked on majorly, obviously on the court, because off the court I'm super relaxed. You never get outbursts. I'm quite chilled out.

"On the court, it's taken a lot of work to get to a point where it's like, this guy, you can clearly tell he's been working on things, he's his own personality, but he's kind of walking a fine line at times but he's worked on it.

"I'm proud of that, that I'm able to play a match like today. There were a couple of outbursts here and there, but it's a kind of maintained mindset."

Cincinnati didn't begin or end well either for World No.2 Rafael Nadal. Returning to the tennis court after withdrawing at Wimbledon, he suffered a shock loss to Croatia's Borna Coric, 7-6 (11-9 tiebreak), 4-6, 6-3 in the second round after a bye in the first.

Kyrgios and Kokkinakis made it to the second round of the doubles after defeating Italian pair Simone Bolelli and Fabio

Fognini 6-0, 6-4 to extend their unbeaten run for the year to five matches, including the Australian Open and Atlanta titles.

But that is as far as they got, although they only narrowly missed getting to the quarter-finals, going down to top seeds Rajeev Ram (US) and Joe Salisbury (UK) 6-7 (3), 6-2, 10-8 after taking the first set in a tie-breaker and forcing the third set into 18 games.

The Kyrgios campaign at Cincinnati was over inside the first week. Next stop, the US Open.

FOOTNOTE: ATP (Association of Tennis Professionals) tour events range from 250, 500 and 1000 ratings, based on rankings points available. The ATP Tour comprises ATP Masters 1000, ATP 500, and ATP 250 tournaments and the ATP Cup. Grand Slams are worth 2000 rankings points. The Davis Cup and the entry-level ITF World Tennis Tour are overseen by the International Tennis Federation (ITF).

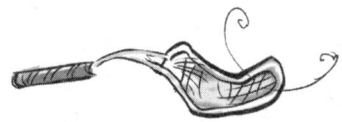

Kyrgios pocketed more than $A 700,000 for his quarter-final appearance at the US Open, adding to his collect earlier in the North American Swing and his $A 1.8 million for being runner-up at Wimbledon.

He would still have considerable change after paying fines that came to $US 32,500 ($A 47,500) at Flushing Meadows, getting penalised five times for offences that included spitting,

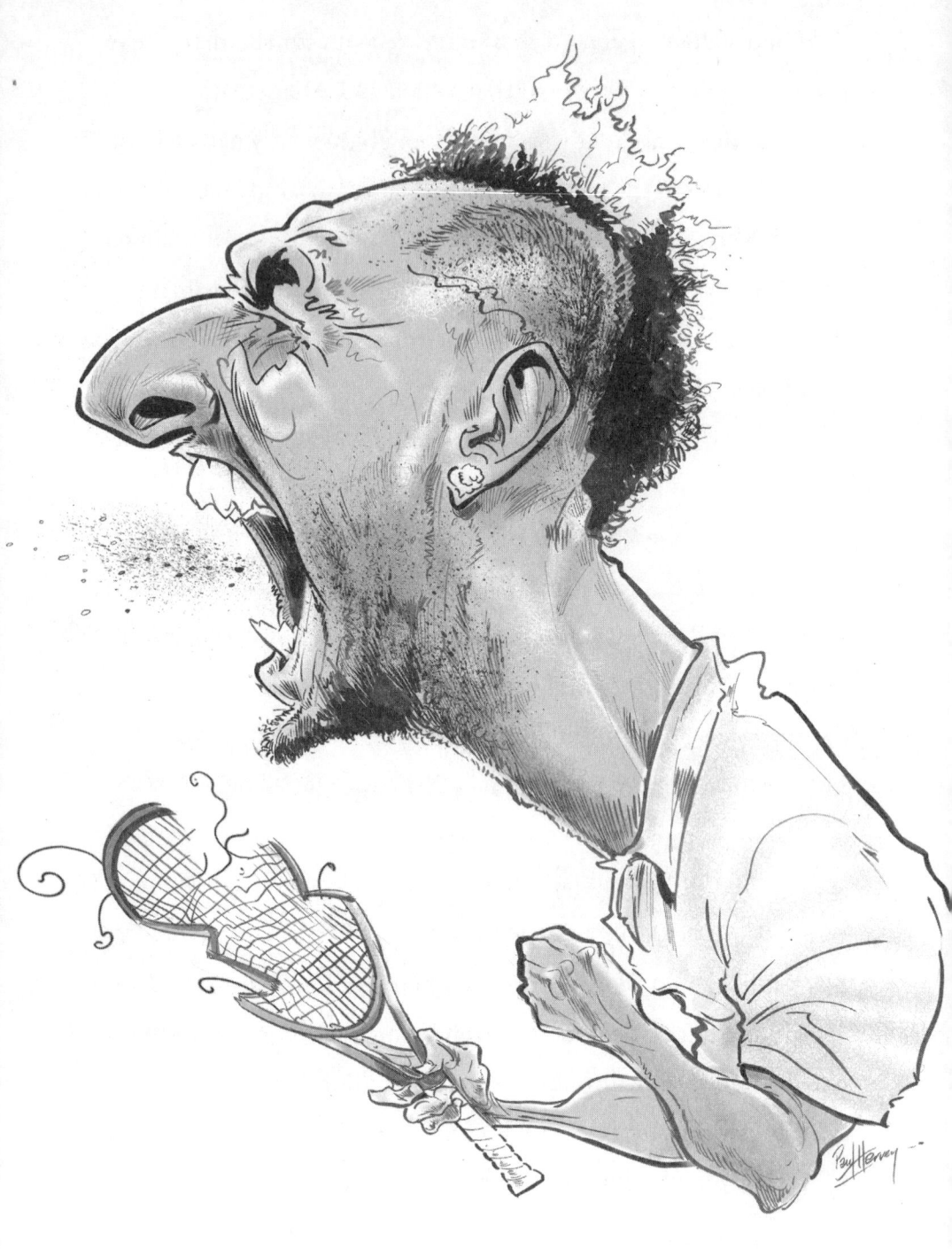

swearing and smashing racquets. He was warned during the third set of the match for throwing a drinks bottle to the ground

An audible obscenity uttered in the Medvedev match cost Kyrgios $US 4,000, his third monetary penalty for the tournament to that point. He copped a $US 7,500 for spitting in his second-round match and another $US 4,000 for racquet abuse during his doubles match with Thanasi Kokkinakis – a total of $US 15,500 ($A25,600).

He was fined $US 14,000 ($A 20,700) for unsportsmanlike conduct after his racquet-smashing exit from the quarter-final.

But he still declared a profit, having earned $US 473,200 ($A 701,700) in prizemoney at the year's final Grand Slam tournament, including a payout for reaching the third round of the doubles with Thanasi Kokkinakis.

As he headed home to Australia, his next court date was likely to be of the legal kind, an assault complaint filed by a former girlfriend.

Another tournament or two before year's end was possible but he was setting his sights on the Australian Open in 2023 where he could have the opportunity for a rematch with his Wimbledon conqueror Novak Djokovic who this time might be allowed to set foot on centre court in Melbourne.

He wasn't playing Davis Cup or Laver Cup, two significant team events remaining on the ATP Tour calendar for the year.

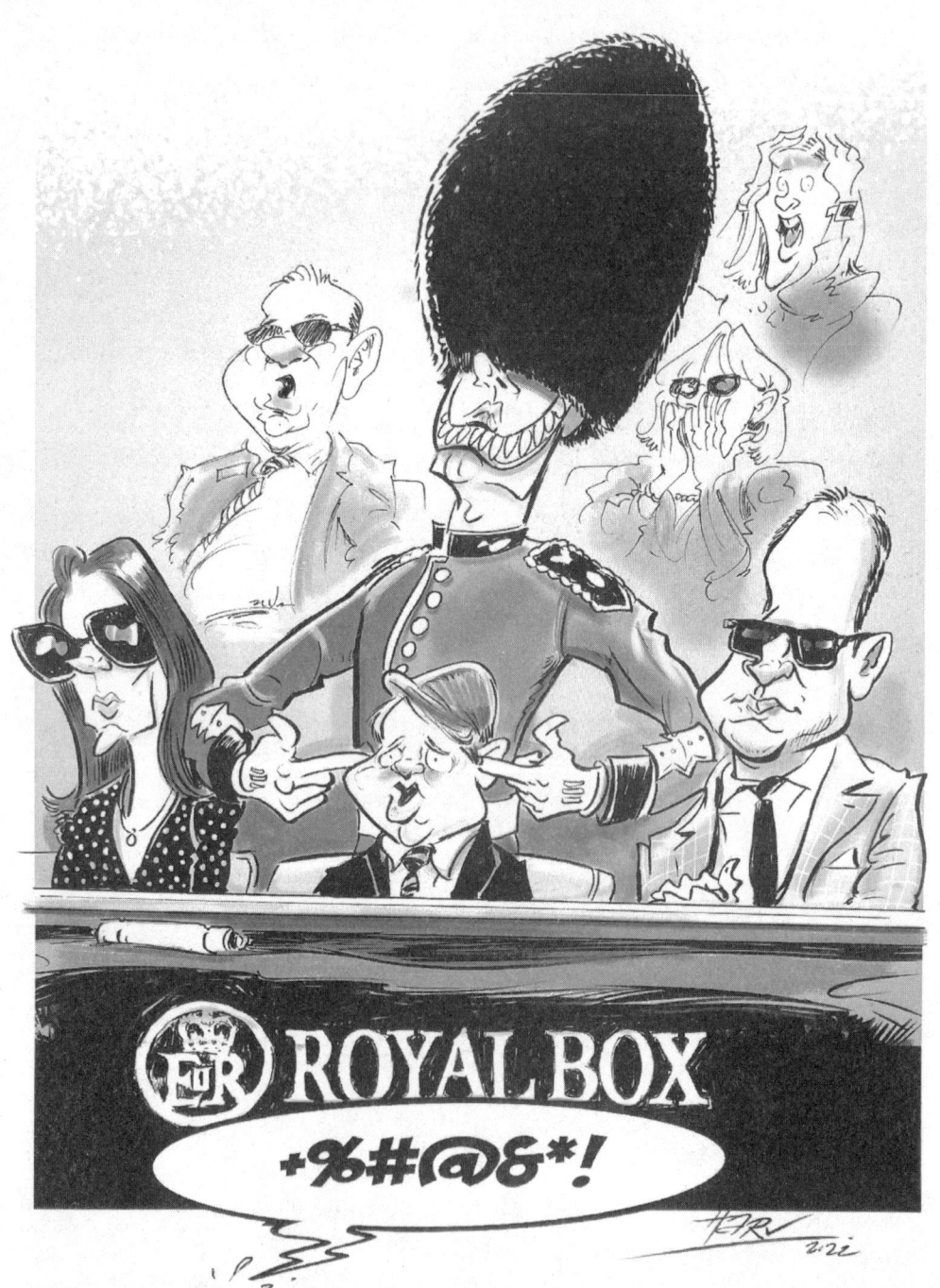

GREATEST HITS

When you go to the tennis to watch Nick Kyrgios play you can never be sure what you will get.

You may get flashes of brilliant tennis. You may see some outlandish behaviour, an underarm serve, a "tweenie", a bullet-like ace, some yelling. Whatever happens, it's bound to be an exciting experience.

Take Wimbledon 2022. One of the first things Kyrgios did was challenge the somewhat antiquated – tradition is still highly regarded – rule of all-white attire on the courts for the All England championship. He turned up wearing bright red shoes and sported a bright red cap on some occasions. Tut, tut went the strawberries-and-cream set.

That Kyrgios would challenge tradition should not surprise. His career is dotted with colorful behaviour, mostly of the language variety, but some more serious.

It would have been interesting to be within earshot of Prince William and Kate – the royal representatives at Wimbledon in 2022 – as little Prince George asked them to explain some of the words from Kyrgios that could be heard close to the court.

It was certainly a colourful education in expressive language for the eight-year-old prince. One can only wonder what the royal reaction might have been months later if George chose some of those words for himself. The audible obscenity cost Kyrgios $A 5,620.

Kyrgios often has paid a price for his antics. The price has ranged from fines to disqualification and suspended sentences.

According to press reports, the Australian had become the most fined player in world tennis, his career total approaching $A 800,000.

If there's a good side to that, the money collected apparently goes back into the sport or to charity; fines imposed by the Grand Slam Board are paid within 10 days and are used to finance the Grand Slam Player Development Program.

The collector of revenue was particularly busy at Wimbledon; even after the last point had been won and the trophies presented, another fine was imposed on the Australian.

Kyrgios's third-round Wimbledon clash with Stefanos Tsitsipas was particularly productive, both players copping the wrath of officialdom for their roles in what was a spiteful clash.

There was no love lost between the pair, a little strange as they once were doubles partners, but their tolerance of each other has been an on-again off-again arrangement since 2018.

Before their match there was no hint of an outbreak of animosity. Both players spoke of their excitement to be facing each other.

"I am definitely thrilled to be facing him," Tsitsipas told reporters. "I respect him a lot, on the court, what he's trying to do. I think he's playing good tennis."

Kyrgios said: "I'm excited. We're two of the biggest stars in the sport. Hopefully if we both bring our best tennis, it's going to be amazing to watch."

In some respects, it was amazing.

Tsitsipas received a warning for smashing a ball into the crowd, apparently almost hitting a spectator. Kyrgios berated the chair umpire for not defaulting his opponent; his persistent complaining led to a warning.

Tsitsipas sought to mete out his own retribution, aiming a number of shots at the Australian and one into the scoreboard.

Kyrgios went on to win the match 6-7 (2/7), 6-4, 6-3, 7-6 (9/7). But the hostilities continued.

Tsitsipas took aim verbally at Kyrgios afterwards: "He has a very evil side to him. It's constant bullying, that's what he does. He bullies the opponents. He was probably a bully at school himself."

Kyrgios's response: Tsitsipas was "soft" and a sore loser.

All that cost both of them money. Kyrgios was fined $A 5,620 for swearing (an audible obscenity) during the match while Tsitsipas was fined $A 14,400 for unsportsmanlike conduct.

Earlier, Kyrgios was embroiled in controversy in his first-round class with Brit Paul Job after spitting towards a fan. That cost him around $A 14,400.

Overall, Wimbledon cost Kyrgios $A 26,347 of his total runners-up prizemoney of $A 1.756 million.

Kyrgios also has been subjected to the biggest fine in world tennis. At the 2019 Western and Southern Open in Cincinnati, he was fined $A 195,500 for five separate incidents including unsportsmanlike conduct in a match against Russian Karen Khachanov.

He was also given a 16-week suspension and had to serve a six-month probationary period.

SOME OF KYRGIOS'S MOST NOTABLE ACTIONS:

Montreal Masters 2015: Sledged Swiss star Stan Wawrinka by telling him fellow Australian Thanasi Kokkinakis had slept with his girlfriend.

Shanghai Masters 2016: Fined for what the ATP described as "Lack of Best Efforts (tanking), Verbal Abuse of a Spectator, and Unsportsmanlike Conduct."

French Open, 2017: Upset after the death of his grandfather, he asked for a beer during a match against South Africa's Kevin Anderson.

Italian Open 2019: He walked off the court after slamming his racquet into the clay, kicking a water bottle and throwing a chair. He was defaulted from his second-round match.

Cincinnati Masters 2019: Umpire Fergus Murphy called him for taking too much time between serves. "That's hilarious. If Rafa (Nadal) plays that quick, I'm retiring from tennis," Kyrgios said, before going on to call Murphy "the worst referee in the game". He walked off the court and smashed two rackets, and later appeared to spit in the direction of the official. That cost him $US 113,000, and a suspended 16-week suspension,

Miami Open, March 2022: He directed a tirade of verbal abuse at umpire Carlos Bernardes and smashed his racquet after a fourth-round loss.

ATP Houston event, April 2022: He launched a tirade at an umpire during a match against American Reilly Opelka after Opelka returned a serve that Kyrgios believed was out.

To finish his visit to North America in 2022, Kyrgios shook hands with his conqueror in the quarter-final of the US Open, thanked the officials, smashed a couple of racquets and walked out of the stadium. Penalties followed. Destroying the racquets cost him $US 14,000, the biggest fine at the US Open. He was penalised five times and fined a total of $US 32,500 during the tournament.

Some incidents in his career probably were more funny than outrageous in terms of breaches of the players' code of conduct.

During his defeat to Roger Federer at the Laver Cup in 2019, Kyrgios was caught by TV cameras saying he had become distracted by a "hot chick in the crowd."

"I lost concentration. I saw a really hot chick in the crowd," Kyrgios said just after the second set. "Like, I'm being jarringly honest – I'd marry her right now. Right now."

He later withdrew from the tournament with an injury. He didn't marry the woman.

One of the weirdest incidents was at Wimbledon in 2015. In an exchange with an online fan, Kyrgios called for fans to smear their faces with Vegemite and Nutella to show their support. Kyrgios posted on Facebook to a fan: "Doesn't get more Australian than support of your locals and a face full of Vegemite." Such is the "woke" movement, the craze sparked a racism debate with fans and players.

The colour of towels was an issue in 2019 during the Rogers Cup (Canada). Kyrgios shouted at the umpire that he wanted white towels, not ones with the tournament brand on them–"I just want to know why it took you so long to get a white towel."

He was bundled out of Wimbledon in round two by Rafael Nadal in 2019. It was later revealed he had been drinking with journalists and "chatting with girls" at in a local pub, *The Dog & Fox*, until 11pm the night before his centre-court match.

MIXING IT WITH THE MEDIA

Few would question that Nick Kyrgios is a significant tennis talent. But many also question the way he goes about things.

He has critics, quite a few as it turns out when you read social media posts and letters-to-the-editor in the press. But few of the critics know the man well and his dislike of some of the media coverage and questions by journalists means the real Nick Kyrgios remains to a large degree concealed. He probably prefers it that way.

Media coverage often precedes the Kyrgios name with such descriptors as "bad boy", "maverick", "polarizing." Rarely, a story begins "tennis star Nick Kyrgios."

He had some comments for and about the media at the Canada Open in August 2022: "I don't care if people don't like me and the style of tennis I play. I understand that. It's more like (at) the beginning of my career, (the media) almost painting an image that completely wasn't me based on what I was doing on the court, which was so hard to disconnect from in real life. None of you understands what that's like, when people just paint an image of how you are as a general human 95% of the time, but you're only seeing me on the tennis court for 2% of my life."

Tour players are obliged to attend media conferences after matches. Nick Kyrgios usually is forthright. After a win he can be relaxed. Not so after a loss. Again, after losing his quarter-final in Canada: "As for media, I couldn't care less. I do this because I have to be here and I don't want to get fined, so I mean, it's routine. I don't really enjoy it, to be honest. I'd rather not be here right now."

Some of his fiercest critics have been former players – fellow Australians Pat Cash and Rennae Stubbs, among the most vocal about his behaviour on court at Wimbledon in 2022. Contemporary players however seem a little more reticent, perhaps out of fear of coming up against him in their next match, perhaps out of understanding the man better than non-players.

Former players (now coaches and commentators) John McEnroe and Lleyton Hewitt these days also seem to have a better understanding of what makes Kyrgios tick.

Fronting the media does not always go well for Kyrgios – or for the media – when the questioning strays from the line Kyrgios would prefer. He would claim that too often the questions don't focus on tennis, that journalists try to bait him on controversial issues.

So, he's not a big fan of the media.

He tweeted in April 2022: "When I see my name of my brothers/sisters names getting spun through the media, I refer to all my research about who they (the media) are. Their job is to CONTROL PUBLIC PERCEPTION, all while profiting off discussing, discrediting and disrespecting people's lives for entertainment."

If he doesn't like a particular line of questioning, the inquisitor can expect short shrift.

At Miami in March 2022, he called the match official "horrendous" and "embarrassing" during several outbursts. That run-in with central umpire Carlos Bernades followed a similar episode earlier in the month at Indian Wells.

At Miami, the first blow-up came when the umpire's walkie-talkie radio came to life during a point in the first set.

There was a further blow-up when Kyrgios was docked a point during a tiebreaker and then a whole game at the start of the second set.

His 29 March press conference after losing to Jannik Sinner began predictably, and possibly with some trepidation on the part of the person who began proceedings:

Q: *I'm sure you know what we are going to ask you about. You had spoken the other day about being more at peace, being more calm. What happened out there on the court during the singles match?*

NICK KYRGIOS: I got frustrated. Can I not get frustrated? Do you get frustrated? Are you at peace in your life? Next question.

Later questions returned to his run-in with Bernades, possibly with some baiting involved:

Q. *Just on Carlos Bernardes, have you spoken to the ATP officiating side and asked if it's possible at least for a period not to have him on any of your matches?*

NICK KYRGIOS: Look...

Q. *He's regarded as a very good umpire.*

NICK KYRGIOS: To whom?

Q. *Obviously there are people, you have personality clashes and things like that, as well.*

NICK KYRGIOS: But like who is he a good umpire, like to whom? Like who thinks he's a good umpire? I don't know. But like I'm just saying like I don't think like when everyone in that crowd is booing an umpire, and he's becoming the centre of attention, that's not his job. Because no one in that entire stadium bought a ticket to see him talk or play or do what he does.

Another journalist got short shrift from Kyrgios after he bowed out of the BNP Paribas Open at Indian Wells to Raphael Nadal, in a match where a flying Kyrgios racket just missed a ball boy after he slammed it into the ground.

A journalist waded into deep water:

Q. *You are obviously an emotional player, but are you aware how close you came to hitting the ball boy with your racquet after the match and what, do you have something to say about it?*

NICK KYRGIOS: What would you like me to say about it? Obviously, was that my intention? No. Because I threw the racquet. Did I throw the racquet anywhere near him originally? It landed a meter from my foot and skidded and nearly hit him. I'm human. Things happen like that. Obviously it was a very misfortunate bounce. I think if I did that a million times over it wouldn't have gone that way. And what do you want me to say? It was three meters away from the kid. That's a question you're going to say after a three-hour battle against Nadal? That's what you come here with?

Q. *Well, I saw a kid duck...*

NICK KYRGIOS: He ducked. Duck. He ducked. He ducked. He ducked. He ducked. Jesus. All right.

Well, if that's what you're going to come in here to come ask me, it didn't hit him. It was an accident. It most definitely wasn't like Zverev.

It was a complete accident. I didn't hit him, thankfully. It wasn't my intention. So thankfully the ball kid's okay. Great question, though. Unbelievable stuff. (Clapping.) Congratulations, man.

FOOTNOTE:Kyrgios tracked down the ball boy, apologised and gave him a racquet.(Alexander Zverev was disqualified from the Mexican Open, given a $US 40,000 fine, lost all rankings points and prizemoney and given an eight-month suspended ban after he swung his racket at the chair umpire's stand four times).

The Indian Wells incident cost Kyrgios $US 33,000. At Miami he was penalised on three counts for a total of $US 47,000.

The feud with Bernades started at the beginning of the year, at the Australian Open in January 2022.

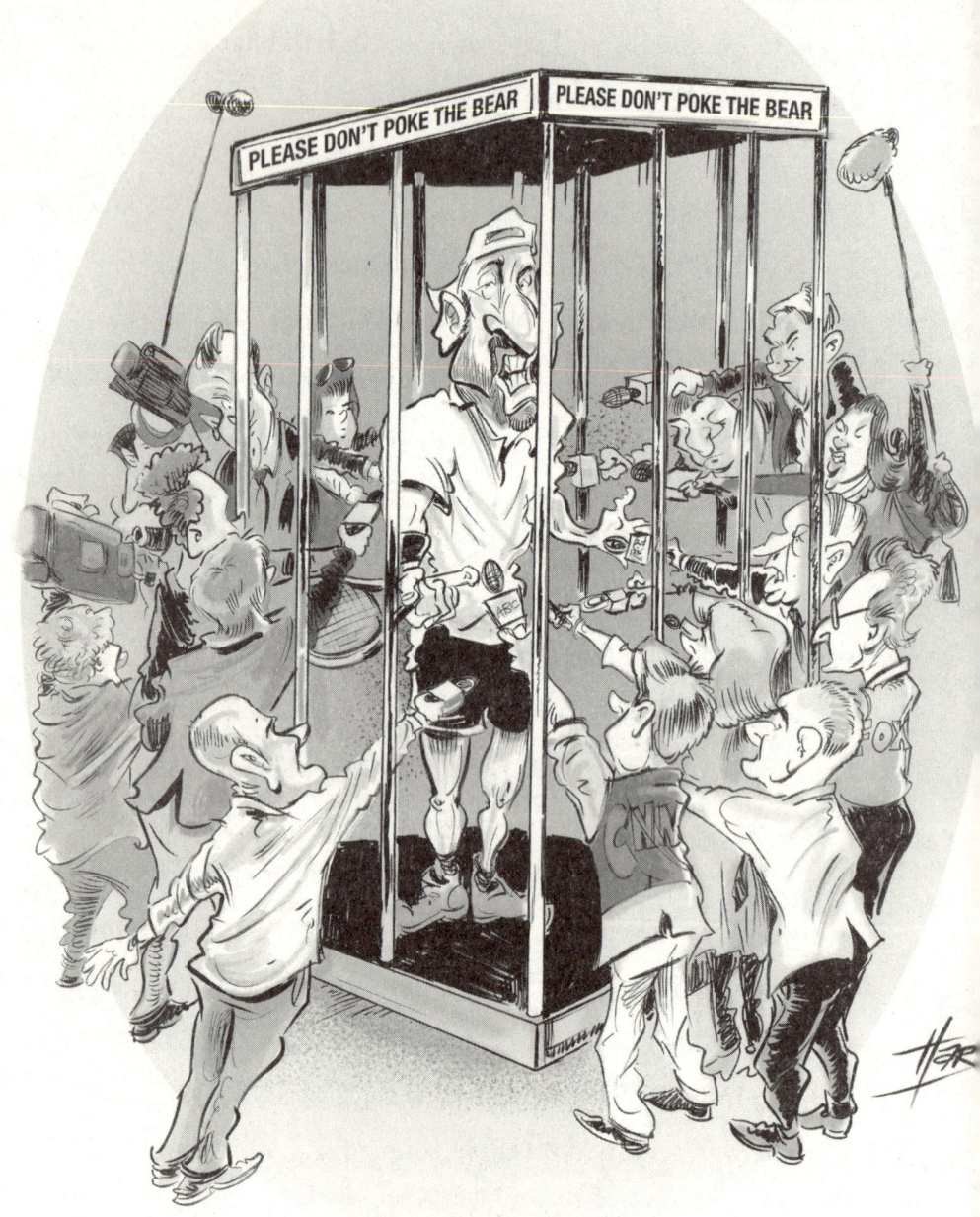

Kyrgios ranted at Bernades during a tense first set when he was playing Russian Daniil Medvedev after he felt he wasn't given enough time to recover after a long point.

"I played a long point, I instantly went to the towel, I came back and there was seven seconds on the clock.

"How is that possible? It can't happen. Otherwise you ruin the match," he raged.

"They're here to watch us, not you, alright. Be reasonable.

"Don't forget this match is about me and him, yeah? Don't ruin it by putting the clock too fast.

"Let the people enjoy without that stupid shit happening, okay?"

There were further spot fires, about crowd noise and the delivery of towels, that saw Kyrgios challenge the umpire again when he was given a time violation.

Bernades seemed to shrug all that off. He wasn't so generous when the Tour left Australia and arrived back in the US.

The Australian Open was a mixed bag for Kyrgios: he went down with Covid before the tournament and lost a tough match to Medvedev. But he joined fellow Australian and mate Thanasi Kokkinakis in defeating fellow Australians Max Purcell and Matthew Ebden in the doubles final (Purcell and Ebden were to have their day on court at Wimbledon later in 2022 when they claimed the doubles championship there.)

The doubles win gave Kyrgios his first Grand Slam trophy. He said afterwards: "I have won some big titles around the world, played some amazing matches. This one ranks (number) one for me."

Kyrgios can be more forthcoming in one-on-one interviews with specialist publications and web sites outside of the mass media, yet a complete profile of the enigmatic Nick Kyrgios requires of lot of piecing together of the parts.

Tidbits can sometimes drop from after-match press conferences once through the "how do you feel line" question is done with, win or lose. Between the start of 2022 and the end of Wimbledon he was involved in around 20 after-match face-to-face sessions with the media – in Australia, the US, France, Paris (where he lost to Raphael Nadal), and England.

We have learned that he doesn't like crowd interaction during matches.

He was asked about it and responded: "I'm not expecting the crowd to go for me. Like, I know when you play Rafa, like, 99 percent of the crowd is going to go for these guys. And I'm not asking for the crowd to go for me or cheer my name or go nuts for me when I'm winning or losing or anything.

"I just want people to know that you're a spectator. You've bought tickets to come watch us play. At least don't scream out before first and second serve. That's all I'm asking for.

"When I was in the Australian Open, before they were screaming, Liam Broady was serving. I told the chair umpire, I was like, tell these guys to shut up. You know what I mean? People in the crowd screaming. And I think it's just this generation. Everyone feels like their opinion is valid. Like, when you're a spectator and you're watching professionals play tennis, you should just be quiet. Do you know what I mean? Like, don't tell me how to play. Like, you could not win a single point guess Rafael Nadal. Just sit on your seat and watch me play tennis. That's it. Period.

"And they think that they have some sort of right to scream out to players like they did to (Naomi) Osaka. Like, it affects people. Like, we're only human. We're not some sort of superhuman with armor. Sometimes I do throw a racquet and it may get close to someone. Like, I'm not perfect, but like, what I'm saying is you can't do that to people. Like, you can't scream out and aggressively scream at people from the crowd. Like, just sit and enjoy the show. Like, we're putting on, I thought it was a decent match. I thought it was a pretty high-level match and I'm just asking for a little bit of respect.

"I'm going out there and competing in the heat for three hours for them. Like, I came out there to play for them. Like, I just want a bit of, like, don't scream out before first and second serve. That's it."

And at Indian Wells we learned a little about his focus:

Q: *I feel like when we watch you play, everybody's different in tennis, everybody has different approaches. We have the impression that if you could just keep your focus at times it could make a difference against someone like Rafa?*

NICK KYRGIOS: Have you played Rafa before?

Q. *No, of course not.*

NICK KYRGIOS: So why, why are you asking me this?

Q. *I wondered whether you...*

NICK KYRGIOS: No, you've implied that I was loose mentally or something today. That's what you implied.

Q. *Not loose mentally...*

NICK KYRGIOS: But how do you know?

Q. *I don't know, that's why I'm asking you.*

NICK KYRGIOS: Well what's your question though?

Q. *Do you think it affects the outcome of the match when you aren't in the same kind of zone where you're focused on what you're doing?*

NICK KYRGIOS: But I was focused. Just because I have an outburst doesn't mean I'm not focused. Like, to be honest, if I was watching a little kid play and he was getting angry that he was losing it just shows that he cares. I would rather someone get angry that they're losing than just cop it on the chin. Did you ever look at it from that way?

He was asked about motivation and pressure after losing the Wimbledon final.

Q. *How do you think your motivation and belief in yourself will be affected by today and this whole fortnight?*

NICK KYRGIOS: Yeah, I was just speaking to a couple of people about it. I feel like if I had won today, I would have struggled with motivation. I've been told my entire life winning Wimbledon is the ultimate achievement. For someone like me, I'm not like a young guy like Sinner or someone or Carlos Alcaraz, who have come on tour recently and gone deep in slams. I"s taken me 10 years, almost 10 years in my career to finally get to the point of playing for a Grand Slam and coming up short.

I feel like if I had won that Grand Slam, I think I would have lacked a bit of motivation, to be honest. Coming back for other tournaments, like 250s and stuff, I would have really struggled. I kind of achieved the greatest pinnacle of what you can achieve in tennis.

But my level is right there. I feel like you look at what Novak has done to some other opponents, and it's not a good feeling. But I'm right there. I'm not behind the eight ball at all. I played a slam final against one of the greatest of all time, and I was right there.

Confidence obviously. It was a hell of an occasion. People were probably expecting me to have something happen today. But I came out in the first set and I looked like I was the one who had played in a lot of finals. I thought I dealt with the pressure pretty well.

At Wimbledon we also learned that he does things his way. Asked about wearing red trainers and red cap on to the court by a reporter, he gave a straightforward answer.

Q: *We all know the Wimbledon dress code rules are very strict. 'Competitors must be dressed in suitable tennis attire that is almost entirely white and this applies from the point at which the player enters the court surround'. Why then, would you walk onto Centre Court with bright red trainers on and do an interview in a red cap?*

NICK KYRGIOS: "Because I do what I want."

Q: *So you're above the rules?*

NICK KYRGIOS: "No. I'm not above the rules."

Q: *So, what is it? They don't apply to you?*

NICK KYRGIOS: "Well I just like wearing my Jordans."

The reporter's line of questioning also gave some insight into how some in the media go after him, even sounding is if it was a personal affront to the reporter that he wasn't complying with dress rules.

Q: *But there are rules specifically against that. I don't want to spoil the surprise, but the referees are going to be speaking to you about it afterwards.*

NICK KYRGIOS: "That's OK. I wear some Triple Whites tomorrow."

Q: "That's fine then. So everyone else in both draws follows the rules but Nick Kyrgios doesn't?"

NICK KYRGIOS: "But nobody else, even after Wimbledon, no-one else really walks with Jordans on the court."

Q: *But, sorry, Nick has just moaned about the controversy that surrounds him...*

NICK KYRGIOS: "I haven't moaned. I love it."

Q: *But you've laughed it off. So, that's all part of it you reckon?*

NICK KYRGIOS: "Well yeah, it's more attention for me. What's that saying? Any publicity is good publicity. Right?"

Q: *If you say so.*

NICK KYRGIOS: "Keep doing you then champion."

Trying to bait Kyrgios seems to be a challenge for some reporters. One reporter questioned him about the intervention of a protestor during the Wimbledon final. He told her he liked that she tried to bait him.

The reporter asked Kyrgios whether he was distracted during the match when Australian human rights activist Drew Pavlou disrupted play to protest. (Mr Pavlou, an anti-communist activist who ran unsuccessfully for election to the Australian Senate, was protesting over the whereabouts and wellbeing of Chinese women's tennis player Peng Shuai). The reporter asked Kyrgios what he thought about people protesting during a match, "especially when it relates to a Chinese tennis player."

Kyrgios simply said he "didn't get distracted at all."

"Can you tell us what happened?" she asked in a follow-up question.

"I didn't hear or see anything. I just saw a couple of people on each other, and they got taken out," Kyrgios replied. But I like that you were trying to bait me, I like that. Good try, good, good try."

We gained a little more insight into his approach to tennis when interviewed on Channel Nine's *Wide World of Sports* program.

"Look at the matches I played, it's exciting, it's focused, it's still a bit different," he said. "It's something I struggle to deal with, the balance. I've always been like that since I was a kid. Matches were always a rollercoaster. I don't know, I'm never going to be someone who goes out there and ticks all the boxes.

"I really try hard. It's a struggle for me sometimes; some days to wake up and come to the courts or wake up and just not want to leave my room. I deal with normal human issues but I'm also just proud of myself that I go out there and keep my head down and I play well. It's not easy to do week in and week out."

He said he was "two very different people on the court, off the court".

Persistent questions about news that he had been directed to appear in court in Canberra on an assault matter were, perhaps surprisingly, met with a straight bat, as they'd say in another sport.

He conceded his road to Wimbledon had been "rocky" when

repeatedly questioned about the court summons in a post-match press conference. But he said he was advised by his lawyers not to discuss the matter.

"Obviously, I have a lot of thoughts, a lot of things I want to say, kind of my side about it," he said. "Obviously, I've been advised by my lawyers that I'm unable to say anything at this time.

"Look, I understand everyone wants to kind of ask about it and all that, but I can't give you too much on that right now."

He faced questions again in Montreal at the Canada Open about his prospects of beating top players as he prepared to face World No. 1 Daniil Medvedev in a second-round match.

His response: "You guys are acting like I haven't beaten World No. 1s before. I've beaten Medvedev before. I've beaten Roger, Novak, Rafael. Like I feel like my confidence and my belief in myself is never short. I could lose five matches in a row and I still believe I have a chance to beat anyone."

He went on to beat Medvedev.

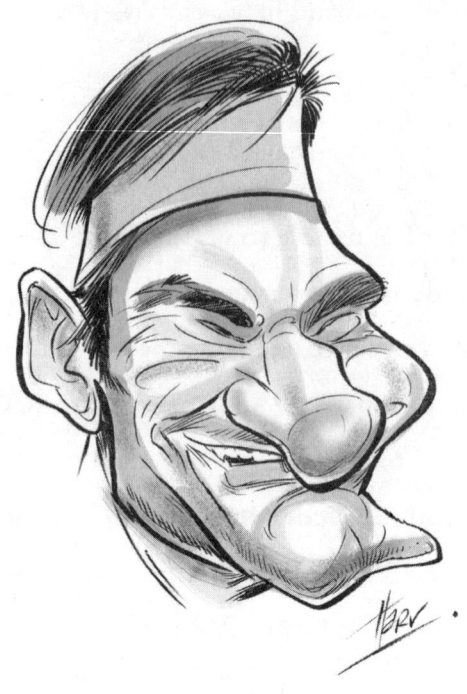

"I'd rather not play five-set matches against Nick because they would last too long and we would probably both grow beards before the end."

ROGER FEDERER

LOVED OR LOATHED

Always someone to go against the grain, Nick Kyrgios oozes a burning competitive streak that has seen him become involved in rivalries with opponents. He has as much knack for rubbing them the wrong way, as they do of him. These rivalries have fuelled the fire within Kyrgios, good and bad.

Tennis is an enthralling sport when two stars won't take a backward step. You can feel the unbridled wrath burning inside. Not only do they want to win and progress forward, but they also want to eviscerate their opponent mentally.

The War between Nick Kyrgios and Stefanos Tsitsipas is like something out of Homer's Iliad. The matches between these former friends are anything but cordial. It is an all-out war. In what can only be described as a turbulent relationship, Kyrgios and Tsitsipas are more like Sid and Nancy than Romeo and Juliet. Once doubles partners, they played in one of the most heated Tennis matches in history at Wimbledon 2022.

In a match described as a blockbuster, the Wimbledon crowd was left in eager anticipation as to what would happen when the two met to shake hands after the fiery encounter. What followed was described as the worst handshake in Tennis history, which left Kyrgios bewildered in his post-match press conference saying, "Every time I've lost... I looked people in the eye and I say, Well done today, you were the better man, and he wasn't man enough to do that today."

The fuse sparked between Tsitsipas and Kyrgios lit up the

post-match press conference, engulfing the media and fans alike.

Seven-time Grand Slam Champion, now commentator, Mats Wilander didn't mince his words about the fiery clash speaking on Eurosport saying, "I've never seen anything like it. I'm not sure I want to see something like that, again, to be honest, because I don't think this is what we want to promote in tennis. We want to not promote it as entertainment. We want to promote it as inspirational, educational, but this is what people maybe want to see. I'm not sure I'm a big fan of what's going on to be honest."

Later in his own press conference, Tsitsipas accused Nick of being a bully saying "it's constant bullying, that's what he does. He bullies the opponents. He was probably a bully at school himself. I don't like bullies. I don't like people that put other people down. He has some good traits in his character, as well. But when he also has a very evil side to him, which if it's exposed, it can really do a lot of harm and bad to the people around him."

Kyrgios' reply was straight and brutal and delivered the perfect sledge without an ounce of remorse saying "I don't know what to say. I'm not sure how I bullied him. He was the one hitting balls at me, he was the one that hit a spectator, he was the one that smacked it out of the stadium, I did nothing towards Stefanos Tsitsipas today that was disrespectful. I was not drilling Stefanos Tsitsipas with balls. To come in here and say I bullied him, that's just soft. We're not cut from the same cloth. I go up against guys who are true competitors."

Many pundits, teammates, opponents, and coaches have said

a lot about Kyrgios over the years, here below are some of the best quotes about Australia's firebrand.

"To me, he's always been very kind and generous. He was supporting me after Wimbledon last year, before the US Open, so the way he's been with me, yeah, he's been really nice. People definitely want to watch Nick" – Emma Raducanu (British former US Open winner).

"Kyrgios is a player who has enormous talent, could be winning grand slams or fighting for the No. 1 ranking. He lacks respect for the crowd, his opponent and towards himself." – Rafael Nadal.

"I'd rather not play five-set matches against Nick because they would last too long and we would probably both grow beards before the end." – Roger Federer.

"Nick can play with chaos going on. Not many people can, but he can. We've seen it at the Australian Open in the doubles when it was a big scene like that, that is when he plays his best tennis. His opponents have to be prepared for that." – Lleyton Hewitt.

"You cannot prepare a match against Nick Kyrgios. Nick Kyrgios is a genius, tennis genius. He doesn't know what he's going to play next in the point. We just concentrate what Novak has to do." – Goran Ivanisevic (Novak Djokovic's coach).

"That 40-0 game, he would probably be very upset with himself for losing that game. I didn't win it, he lost that game with his unforced errors. I stayed there, pushed him to the limit and got the reward." Novak Djokovic after defeating Kyrgios in the 2022 Wimbledon Final.

"Honestly, as a tennis fan, I'm glad that he's in the finals because he's got so much talent. Everyone was praising him when he came on the tour, expecting great things from him. For the quality player that he is, this is where he needs to be, and he deserves to be." – Novak Djokovic again.

"He's a good kid, the players like him, he's well liked in the locker room, he does a lot of charity work. But he's got demons you know, in a way – we all have this fear of failure and it's a question of how we best deal with it." – John McEnroe.

"I don't mind people getting upset at a line call, or questioning something or smashing a racket, that's going to get it out of your system, but I think it's the constant stuff that opponents have to deal with. Kids are watching, man, they can hear things, they've got the mics on the court ... you have to think about these things." – Mark Philippoussis (former Australian player).

"Nick's one of the nicest guys out there. He's that person that's always going to have your back, no matter what. I've been fortunate enough to be in Davis Cup ties with him and get to know him better and play side by side with him and he's one of those guys that has always had a lot of confidence in me and has always, from basically a junior, telling me to believe in myself and to go out there and take it. He's very misunderstood but he's one of the nicest guys out there and he'll always have your back. We're almost brothers – pretty close." – Alex De Minaur.

"I think it's a horrible thing. I think breaking a racket on a tennis court is a low-level gesture, because most people can't afford to buy one.

Lleyton Hewitt told me that children in Australia are starting to style themselves like Kyrgios. I'm not saying they throw rackets on every occasion, but they often send the ball off the court like Kyrgios. This is serious enough. Nick is very talented, but he doesn't use his head. He never uses his feet when he hits the ball, but many guys admire him." – Mats Wilander

"I don't think he is a villain at all. I really enjoy watching him play. When he tries hard, he is one of the best players in the world; most probably he still has his best tennis ahead of him. I still feel that he has a big shot at winning a big tournament, especially on the grass at Wimbledon. I don't think he's a villain; I think he's a really nice guy and he is entertaining the crowd. I think it (antics) is just him; some players get upset, some players get nervous. I'm not sure what he's feeling on the inside, but he cares about winning tennis matches and I think that is why he is so emotional at times, but it is fun to watch, and he is a crowd favourite wherever he goes." – Mats Wilander again.

As explosive as he is on the Tennis court, Kyrgios's quotes are complex. They are ranked in the category of *The Good, The Bad, and The Ugly*, after Sergio Leone's famous Spaghetti Western Film starring Clint Eastwood.

THE GOOD.

"It's more attention for me. What's that saying? Any publicity is good publicity, right? I sit here now in the quarter-finals of Wimbledon again, and I just know there's so many people that are so upset. It's a good feeling." – Another famous clash with the media resulted in

Kyrgios celebrating his own achievements at Wimbledon.

"I just feel like I'm comfortable in my own skin. Some people love to just tear me down, but it's just not possible anymore." – Positive comments about his own image, and how he has grown as a human during Wimbledon in 2022.

"We definitely have a bit of a bromance now, which is weird." Quote on Novak Djokovic after the 2022 Wimbledon Final.

"I decided that I needed to play for something bigger than Nick Kyrgios and I decided to start the NK foundation, I tried to really just put everything I do into just giving and helping and just trying to do good every day and that's what drives me to play now." – Kyrgios talking about why he started the NK Foundation.

"I've been playing the same way since I was 10 years old. People think that I'm trying to act that way out there but anyone who that knows me, any of my close mates and anyone that's watched me play... (knows) nothing's really changed." – Kyrgios's comments on the way he plays the game.

"If ANYONE is not working/not getting an income and runs out of food, or times are just tough... please don't go to sleep with an empty stomach. Don't be afraid or embarrassed to send me a private message. I will be more than happy to share whatever I have. Even just for a box of noodles, a loaf of bread, or milk. I will drop it off at your doorstep, no questions asked!" – This statement was posted on Kyrgios' Instagram during the Coronavirus Crisis in 2020, where he publicly offered to

help those who were hit the hardest financially across the pandemic.

"I've been that floater my whole career. Players know that whether I'm seeded or not the ball's kind of out of their court. If I'm confident and playing well, they can't really do much. I'm 60 in the world but feel like I'm top 10 always."– Comments about potentially not being seeded at the 2022 US Open.

"Honestly, I feel as if my first slam final was impressive, next time I would try ride the emotional wave a little smoother, but I realise how much was on the line. I feel if I was up against anyone else but Djokovic in the final, the way I served, I would of won."
– Post-match after the 2022 Wimbledon Final.

"It's hard, there's a lot of things people don't see. They only see me winning, losing, throwing a racquet, doing those things. They don't really understand the challenges that I face or what people on tour face, what's going on in their personal lives." – After defeating World Number 1 Daniil Medvedev at the Canadian Open in 2022.

"It's hard because even travelling now, my mum is in hospital at the moment, my dad hasn't been very well, my brother just had a baby, and I don't get to be there with my family when normal people would like be there with them."– Kyrgios' follow-up quote from his win over Medvedev, showing a softer side to the audience, and explaining the struggles that his family and himself are facing.

THE BAD.

"I just feel like he (Djokovic) has a sick obsession, wanting to be liked. He just wants to be like Roger (Federer). He just wants to be liked so much that I just can't stand him. This whole celebration thing (blowing kisses to the crowd) that he does after matches, it's like so cringeworthy. It's very cringeworthy."
– Kyrgios on Djokovic back in 2019.

"I'm on court and I can't play because I'm a bit horny, if you know what I mean." – Kyrgios reveals his sexual frustration about being on the ATP tour in 2021.

"I'm good in the locker room. I've got many friends, just to let you know. I'm actually one of the most liked. I'm set. Hes not liked. Let's just put that there." – Kyrgios on Tsitsipas after their infamous Wimbledon match in 2022.

"Let's get that water bottle thing clear, it was bad and I shouldnt have done it with kids watching so make sure you put it in the article... My girlfriend will kill me if I don't apologise and it was unacceptable... Denis Shapovalov gets fined $5k for hitting an umpire in the eye and sending him to hospital. I get fined $15k for playing with a water bottle." – Kyrgios's apology after simulating a sex act at during the Semi-Final of the Fever-Tree Championship in 2018.

"I'm two completely different people on and off the court. Like, on the court I'm just literally, I can't explain it, I'm just mental. Really competitive, like sickly obsessed with just putting on a show and

winning. But then off the court, I'm very chilled out." – A great insight into the duality of Kyrgios.

"Are you good at tennis? No. Then why are you speaking? Do I tell him how to act?" – Nick Kyrgios to Ben Stiller (not even famous celebrities are sheltered from Kyrgios' wicked tongue).

THE UGLY.

"I lost concentration. I saw a really hot chick in the crowd... Like, I'm being jarringly honest – I'd marry her right now. Right now." – Kyrgios's response to why he lost concentration playing Swiss great Roger Federer in the 2019 Laver Cup

"Kokkinakis banged your girlfriend. Sorry to tell you that, mate." – No way to tippy-toe around this comment. Not Kyrgios's finest moment. He delivered this brutal sledge to Swiss star Stan Wawrinka during a heated Rogers Cup match in Montreal.

"Get me a beer now. Honest to God, get me one now." – An unusual request from Kyrgios mid match at Roland Garros in 2017, before losing to South African Kevin Anderson in the second round.

"She's drunk out of her mind in the first row, talking to me in the middle of the game, the one with the dress, the one who looks like she's had about 700 drinks, bro!" – Kyrgios's slow descent into madness during the Wimbledon Final, albeit a funny interaction.

"Of one of the people disrespecting me, yes. I would not be doing that to someone who was supporting me, I've been dealing with hate and negativity for a long time, so I don't feel like I owed that.

person anything." – Kyrgios talking about an incident with a fan at Wimbledon during his first round clash with crowd favourite Brit Paul Jubb at Wimbledon in 2022.

"What does that even mean? I'm good at hitting a tennis ball at the net. Big deal. I don't owe them anything. If you don't like it, I didn't ask you to come watch. Just leave." – Kyrgios after a messy Shanghai Masters exit in 2016.

"It's not always easy. It's so accessible now to go on your phone, social media, Twitter, Instagram and just go to messages and comments and you see so much negativity. You may not take it in but subconsciously it's still going into your brain and dealing with hecklers." – Nick Kyrgios *Coming Out of the Darkness*, by Craig Gabriel.

"Has one person today come to see her speak? "No. I understand, but why is she doing that? Not one person in the stadium has come here to watch her do anything! Not one person. Like, you know what I mean? You got fans, but she has got none. What did I do? Like, come on. I know, but what? She just selfishly walks to you in the middle of a game because she's a snitch!"
– Nick Kyrgios berates a linesperson at Wimbledon in 2022.

"The worst f***king ref ever, the worst ref in the game. I've never experienced anything like this in my life. It's a disgrace. It's only with you. Why do I always have problems with this potato in the chair? He's a spud. You're a f***king tool bro." – Fair to say chair umpire Fergus Murphy is not on Kyrgios's Christmas card list after his explosion at the Cincinnati Masters in 2019.

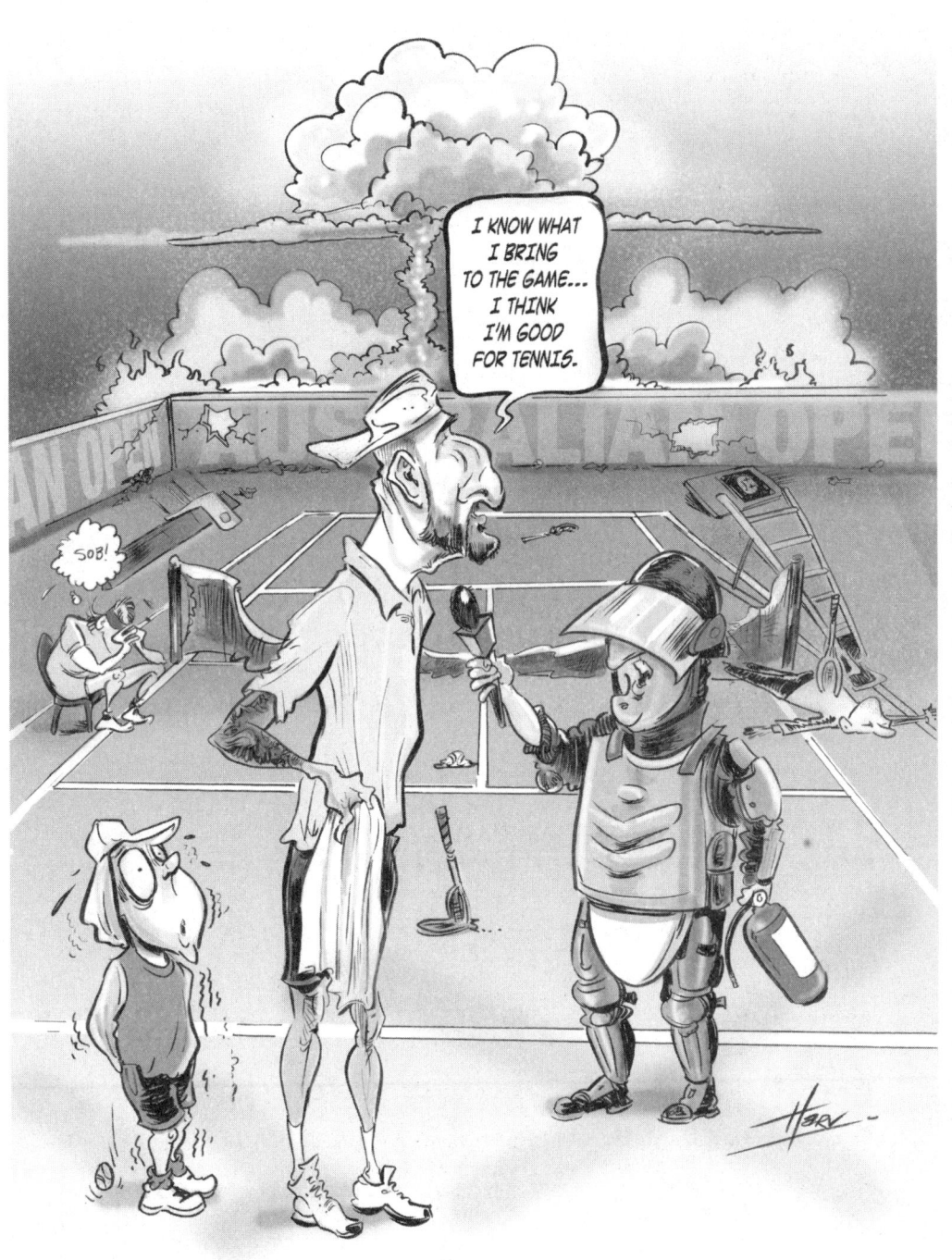

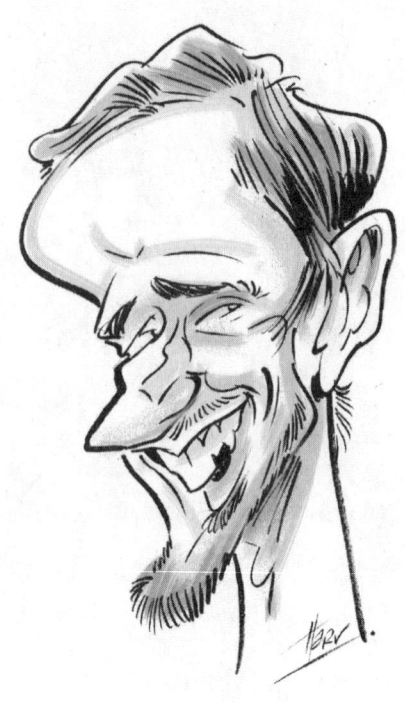

"He has a little bit different game because he's not like a grinder in a way. At the same time he can rally. He's tough to play. He has an amazing serve. He plays good. He has every shot. If he plays like this... he has all the chances to win it."

DANIIL MEDVEDEV

difference now. I see it on his stories. It's probably the first time he's been to Big Ben. All the times he's been to London, he hasn't gone anywhere.

"Since the Australian Open this year (2022), he has started doing some things. Because he now understands that life doesn't revolve around tennis. No one expects him to be like that. You have to enjoy your life. I'm really happy he is now."

Speaking after his triumph in the Citi Open in Washington in August 2022, Kyrgios gave an insight into his liking for the capital and how he valued his free time.

"My home town, Canberra, is basically modelled off this place. It's the same design, honestly, same kind of feel, to be honest, as well. When I'm in Washington, I kind of feel like it's home. It's not as busy as, say, New York or Atlanta or Miami. It's a bit more almost timid-like. It's quiet, a lot of greenery. Feels like home," he said.

"I really enjoyed it. We had a couple days at the start of the tournament when we were doing some sightseeing, so enjoyable, added some great restaurants. Just had a great time. Obviously maybe not as much free time as we would have liked. Obviously my partner and I want days where we can kind of go on dates and see the world, but a week like this, I have been pretty occupied.

This new approach also was evident when he went to New York for the US Open, he and Costeen were photographed on various sightseeing trips around the city.

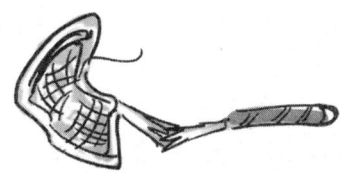

Nick (the youngest), Christos and their sister Halimah are the children of Norlaila and Giorgos Kyrgios.

Norlaila ("Nill") Kyrgios is a Malaysian-born computer engineer. Originally a princess born into a Malaysian Selangor royal family, from Gombak, she dropped her title (Tengku of Pahang, or princess of the Pahang state) and moved to Australia when in her 20s.

Nick's father Giorgos ("George") is a self-employed house painter from Greece. The Kyrgios family settled in Canberra, the Australian capital.

Christos has alopecia and Nick is said to be very protective of him. Christos has worked as a fitness trainer and gym instructor. He is engaged to Alicia Gowans and they recently had a baby, George.

Halimah is a trained dancer and a professional singer. She has been part of *The Voice Australia* talent quest television program. Latest biographical notes say she works in dance and musical theatre and as a voice and performance coach based in Hong Kong.

Norlaila Kyrgios has heart (and more recently kidney) problems, the reasons she doesn't watch her son play. She told an interviewer: "I don't watch Nick play. I'm just too nervous. I get too scared. I'm just hopeless – I tend to hide."

Her heart condition is serious and the family was most concerned for her wellbeing during the Covid outbreak, Nick even calling for the 2021 Australian Open tournament to be cancelled to avoid the possibility of the family being caught up in the pandemic indirectly and the complications his mother could face if she caught the virus.

Giorgos Kyrgios was in Nick's team at Wimbledon, but his mother stayed at home and didn't watch any of his matches, including the final.

"I actually didn't watch the game, she told Channel Nine's Today show. "I haven't watched any of his games.

"I had a very good sleep ... I actually watched him go on court. I love that, you know, watching him walking through Wimbledon, just that atmosphere. I love watching him walk on to the court and just see the reaction of the spectators.

"I watched it until I think when they started warming up and I said, 'Good luck' and I went to bed."

She said watching from the player's box wasn't always a good experience.

"You don't want to be in his box, you really don't, because you really don't know when to stand and when to clap and when to shout.

"We have been there, and it is not a good experience."

She watched a replay of the Wimbledon final though and remained confident that her son could one day be a Grand Slam champion.

"It was a big occasion for him. He doesn't do things in steps, not a gradual process. It is just one minute you are playing first round, the next minute you are in the finals of the biggest slam in the world.

"I think the next time he is there he might use that as

experience and maybe he will be a bit better."

In August 2022, Kyrgios announced he wasn't playing in the Laver Cup team competition after the US Open so he could be at home with his family as his mother battled kidney problems.

He pressed on with his North American hardcourt campaign as his mother was in hospital back in Australia. He signed off his post-match interview after defeating World No. 1 Daniil Medvedev in Montreal by wishing the best to his mother in a message scribbled on a TV camera lens.

After defeating fellow Australian Alex De Minaur, in the following round at Montreal, Kyrgios conceded he was feeling the effects of such a long time on the road.

"These days are starting to blend into one another," he said. "I'm just kind of playing the game, physio, eat, sleep, play. It's tiring, but that's the sport. I am missing home a little bit, I'm not going to lie.

"I've got my mum and my dad, I haven't seen (them) in about three months. So I'm missing home but at the same time I know that it's only a couple of tournaments before I go (back)."

Then, after losing in his quarter-final to Pole Hubert Hurkacz, he said he had struggled physically in the lead-up while his mind had also been on his sick parents back in Australia.

The Australian was not too fussed about losing his first singles match in 10 outings as he spoke again about his parents.

"I honestly don't care (about the winning streak ending)," he said. "I have been on the road for nearly three months and I've been away from home, away from my mum who is in hospital, away from my dad. They're not very well at the moment. So I don't really care about no winning streak.

"When I am on the road I just want to put in good performances and make it worthwhile being here. I don't care about records and that sort of stuff. I just want to make the most of my trip."

His brother Christos, who regularly supports his brother from the stands, confessed watching was sometimes an "uncomfortable" experience.

"He wouldn't be our Nick if he wasn't fiery during the match, and that's how he plays, that's how he gets himself up," he explained.

"He tries to increase his intensity and whatever else and that's how he does it, and that's what we know from him. The fight was there the whole match, the match was incredible.

"You need a pressure valve, right?

"And the pressure valve for him is, 'Look, these people love me, I'm not saying anything to offend or to abuse them, but I just need to release some of that pressure, deflect a bit of that pressure so I can get back down to focusing on what I'm doing'.

"We have said to him many times, 'If you need to, if that helps you in that moment, if it helps you deal with the adversity and the pressure, throw some our way. We're not going anywhere. We are here for you, if it makes it easier for you'."

The rise of Nick Kyrgios to Wimbledon finalist brought his

parents into the limelight to some degree although they generally maintain a low profile. Some biographical notes merely describe Giorgos as the father of "a very famous Australian tennis player."

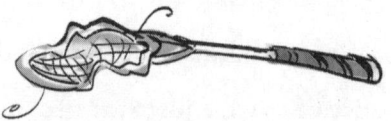

His family acknowledges that Kyrgios's girlfriend Costeen Hatzi has had a positive effect on his life.

She was at courtside for his Wimbledon campaign in 2022. Media reports described her as a Sydney-based blogger and influencer, the pair dating for several months in the lead-up to Wimbledon. They went to the Bahamas together after the tournament. Kyrgios has a house there.

Hatzi, who has almost 100,000 followers on Instagram, also posted tributes to Kyrgios throughout the tournament.

According to *Marie Clair* magazine, she has her own business, Casa Amor Interiors, which sells minimalist, on-trend interior decorations.

The most controversial of his relationships was the one before Costeen Hatzi, with Chiara Passari. It ended acrimoniously, in December 2021; so acrimoniously that Kyrgios found himself facing a complaint of common assault arising from their split.

The pair began dating in 2020 but they split up after an argument in October 2021 that resulted in a police visit to their Adelaide hotel during quarantine. Passari made a report of common assault in December 2021 and it was revealed just before his Wimbledon showdown the following July that Kyrgios would face Canberra magistrates court later in 2022. Passari made it clear she had nothing to do with the timing of the news.

Little more was known of the incident at that time; Australian Capital Territory police said only that a 27-year-old man from the Canberra suburb of Watson was scheduled to face the ACT Magistrates Court in relation to one allegation of common assault. He wasn't required to attend early hearings in person.

Passari and Kyrgios paired just a couple of months after his relationship with Russian tennis player Anna Kalinskaya ended, in May 2020.

Asked about his break-up with Kalinskaya, he conceded that when he was not in a relationship, he regularly slept with female fans.

"Yeah, in all seriousness, if I'm not seeing someone, it's a weekly thing," he was quoted as saying by Melbourne's *Herald Sun* newspaper.

Another previous girlfriend is Australian tennis player Ajla Tomljanovic. Ajla was from Croatia and took Australian nationality in 2018. They met in 2015 and were together through 2016 and until 2017 when injury knocked Kyrgios out of Wimbledon and he was seen partying at a London nightclub with several women. Their relationships ended at that point.

The first question Tomljanovic faced in her post-match press conference at Wimbledon in 2022 had nothing to do with her impressive campaign, or her heartbreaking 6-4, 2-6, 3-6 defeat by Elena Rybakina after threatening a boilover when she took the first set.

Instead, she was asked about Kyrgios and the court matter. She replied: "I'm not really aware of exactly what's being said about whatever his past relationship and the allegations. I don't know what it is.

"I'm definitely against domestic violence. I hope it gets resolved. But yeah, I mean I haven't had that experience with him."

Later, Tomljanovic tweeted: "Quite disappointing that after almost 2 hours of playing my quarter-finals that that was the first question the journalist chose to ask me, and never proceeded to ask anything match related. Glad to see headlines mostly about that now. Do better."

THE DARK SIDE

"I get so angry, I just go through so many different patches in a game. It's so hard for me to find that balance. It's a tug-of-war all the time."

There's more to Nick Kyrgios than meets the eye, even though what's on show is probably plenty – even more than enough – for some tennis fans.

Behind the outgoing show that can range from disrespect, bad language, abuse of officials to plain boorish behaviour, there have been personal battles that are not always understood or explained.

That's not to excuse bad behaviour – its more about understanding the man and his makeup.

As well as whoever is across the tennis net, Kyrgios also has had his battles with his own demons –mental illness.

His chief tormentor has been depression.

He has spoken of those dark days that took him to substance abuse and even self-harm. The worst probably was behind him when he went into the final at Wimbledon against Serb Novak Djokovic. He seemed optimistic about that but admitted to some anxiety.

He said he'd "never felt good" but was in a very different space after playing the biggest match of his life and after the anxiety and expectation had subsided.

"It's just a lot mentally. Everyone supporting you, there

are negative comments. There's the pressure of playing finals at Wimbledon – am I going to do good, am I going to behave well for me? There are so many things," Kyrgios said.

"Playing Djokovic is a hard enough task as it is and to go out there, I lost this match but I feel like there's this weight off my shoulders.

"I feel like there's so much weight on my shoulders all the time when I step out on the tennis court. Now it's just released, and I feel amazing.

"This is the best I've felt in two weeks. I was obviously super-excited to be here and I had some high hopes, but I've never felt, to be honest, good.

"I just felt so much pressure. There's so much anxiety and pressure to do things or achieve things and if I don't do well, it's just so much.

"So I feel unbelievable. Like I'm two beers deep."

He revealed that he hardly slept after getting a walkover in the semi-final.

"The anxiety of having that day off from the semi-final, I slept terribly again last night," Kyrgios said.

"I actually think not playing the semi-finals may have done me a bit of a disservice because I was just thinking about it all the time. But that comes with experience, I thought I handled myself well out there."

He revealed in 2018 he had begun working on his mental health, saying he had been talking to two psychologists – one overseas and one in Australia – to help him cope with the rigours of the tennis tour.

"There were times of the year where I wasn't in the best mental health state, so I've got to go out there and just be happy and enjoy myself and tennis. I think when everything lines up in my life, tennis will take care of itself," he said at the time.

"I probably left it a little too long. But I've been doing that and I feel more open about talking about it, I don't feel like I've got to hide that sort of stuff any more."

Of course, Kyrgios is not the first sportsperson to suffer such highs and lows in their career. Nor is he the first Australian tennis player to do so.

Pat Cash, Wimbledon champion in 1987, told of his highs and lows in his book Uncovered (published in 2002). The lows were drugs, drink, depression and anger–behaviour that has been associated with Kyrgios more recently.

These days Cash is a commentator and there were few more strident than him in criticising Kyrgios's conduct in his victory over Stefanos Tsitsipas at Wimbledon in 2022.

As a young boy, Kyrgios said he battled obesity.

Speaking to Tennis Majors, he said: "Every time I see that picture (of him as a quite overweight 9-year-old), it's incredible.

"I look like Manny from *Modern Family* and it's funny thinking that kid could be me. I believe that my example should serve all those children who have been marginalised and at some point surrounded by negative thoughts.

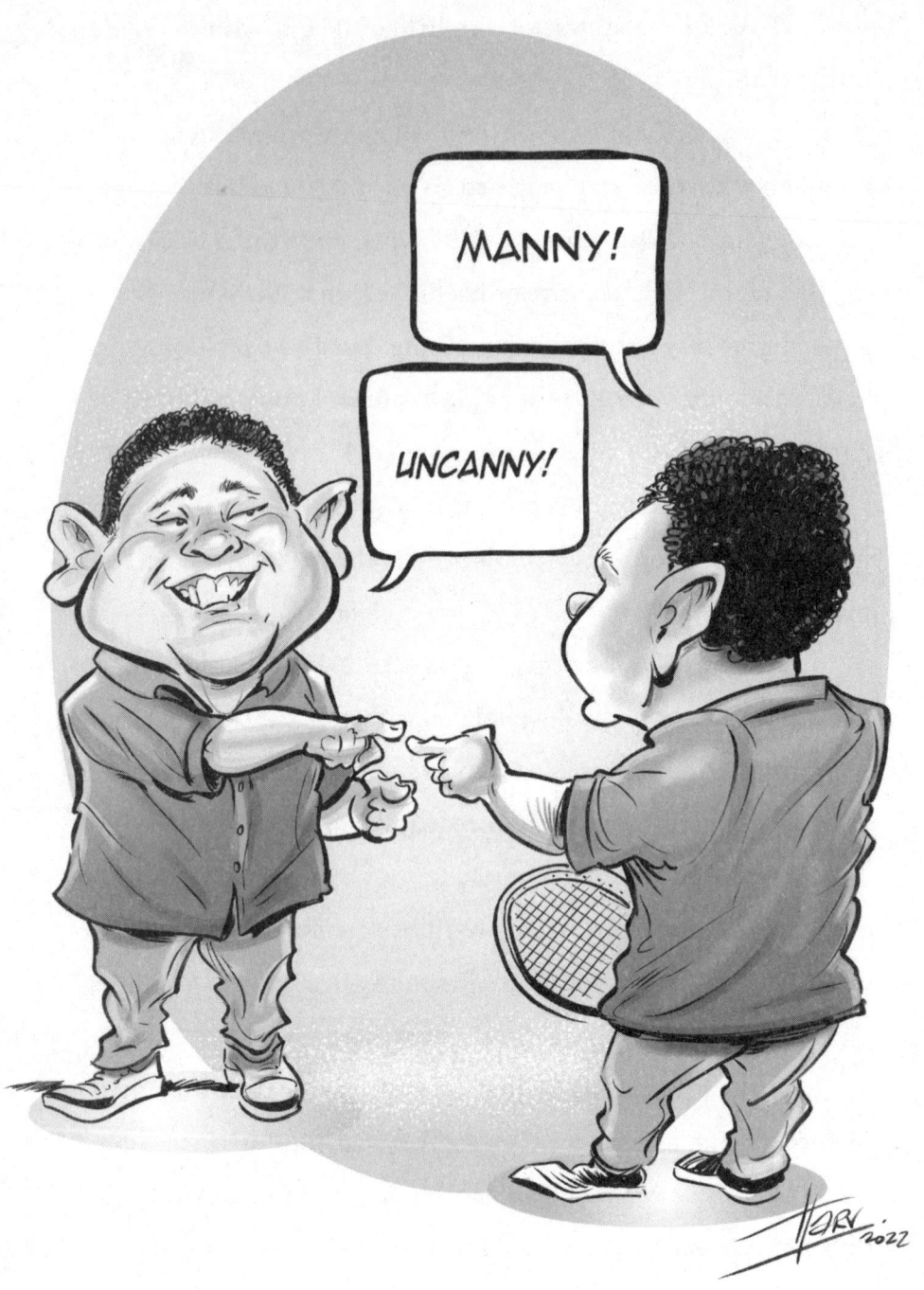

"I convey the idea that, if you have faith in yourself, it is possible to do anything. I have always believed in myself, I have never lost faith despite many doubting my chances."

As his tennis career evolved, Kyrgios's worst year for physical injuries probably was 2018 when he started the season at No. 14, aiming for the top 10. Injuries held him back and he slipped down to No. 38.

He had elbow and arm issues and had to miss many tournaments including the French Open. "It's been a tough year", he said then.

The worldwide Covid epidemic put paid to many international tennis tournaments through 2020 and Kyrgios had precious little court time.

In 2021 an injury to his left knee ended his season early during the Laver Cup. The injury had troubled him for several months. He said in an Instagram post that he was flying home to Australia for treatment.

"Hey guys, over the last couple of months I haven't been near 100% healthy," he posted.

"I've been dealing with left knee patella tendinopathy and continuing to play without fully treating it can lead to further pain and greater setbacks."

Kyrgios had pulled out of Wimbledon earlier that year through an acute abdominal problem during his third-round match with Canadian Felix Auger Aliassime with the scores locked at one-set each.

He had further health problems in the lead-up to the 2022 Australian Open and had to withdraw from the Melbourne Summer Set. Asthma was partly to blame but he also had a knee injury that he said led him to "greater setbacks."

At Wimbledon in 2022, he suffered a shoulder injury in the first set of his last-16 match against American Brandon Nakashima, but this time he battled through five sets to reach the quarter-finals.

"I woke up after Tsitsipas with some shoulder pain," he said afterwards. "I've played so much tennis that I almost thought it was time for my body to start feeling some niggles."

The physiotherapist on his team, Will Maher, is credited with getting Kyrgios through Wimbledon. Maher is a long-time friend as well and is said to have helped Kyrgios adopt a basketball-focused training schedule in the lead-up to Wimbledon.

Kyrgios referred to mental health issues in social media posts in 2022 saying some of his "darkest periods" were around the time of the 2019 Australian Open.

His Instagram post (accompanied by a photo): "Most would assume I was doing OK mentally or enjoying my life... it was one of my darkest periods. If you look closely, on my right arm you can see my self-harm. I was having suicidal thoughts and was literally struggling to get out of bed, let alone play in front of millions. I was lonely, depressed, negative, abusing alcohol, drugs, pushed away family and friends. I felt as if I couldn't talk or trust anyone. This was a result of not opening up and refusing to lean on my loved ones and simply just push myself little by little to be positive. I know that day to day life can seem extremely exhausting, impossible at times. I understand that you feel if you open up it may make you feel weak, or scared. I'm telling you right now, it's OK, you are not alone. I've been through those times when it seemed as if those positive energetic vibes were never ever going to be reality. Please, don't feel as if you are alone, if you feel as if you can't talk to anyone, I'm here, reach out. I'm proud to say I've completely turned myself around and have a completely different outlook on everything, I don't take one moment for granted. I want you to be able to reach your full potential and smile. This life is beautiful."

He added later: "Now, I barely drink, I literally have a glass of wine at dinner. That was the initial kind of thing I had to clean up a little bit and then build my relationship back with my family and get into healthier habits like the basics; diet, getting good sleep, trying to train a little bit more and that was it.

"I think Covid helped me a lot with that," he said acknowledging that he found strength during the lockdowns and was able to cut down on his drinking and build on his relationships with friends and family.

He also encouraged those who might not be okay to reach out and talk to others: "I know that day to day life can seem extremely exhausting, impossible at times," he posted.

Nick Kyrgios's mother, Nill, revealed in a television interview during Wimbledon how fellow tennis player Scot Andy Murray probably helped save her son's life.

She told Channel Nine that while training with the young Australian a few years ago, Murray noticed evidence of self-harm on Kyrgios' body. He told Kyrgios's former manager, John Morris, of his concerns.

"The self-harming... I saw that and people told me that," Nill Kyrgios said.

"I asked him about it and he didn't want to talk about it at that time. John spoke to me that Andy is worried about Nick because he can see some evidence of self-harm... And I blame others for that. For just pressuring him, criticising him. Even people we thought might be supporting him.

"That period was very hard. I just wanted to be next to him constantly so that I could see him. If I could see him I know he's OK. And if I can't see him I worry about him so much that it becomes very difficult."

She told Channel Nine that watching her son's matches put her in such a bad place that she had to seek help for her own mental health.

"I haven't watched him play for a while, actually. I can't expose myself to that anxiety," she said before the Wimbledon final.

But she emphasised her son still had her support. "I am happy. I will celebrate this occasion. Whether he wins or loses, I am super proud that he made it through everything. I'm happy that he's come out well the other end. You just don't know what pressure does to people. It's worrying for a parent."

As well as anxiety, Nill Kyrgios has had another serious health issue to deal with. In 2002 doctors told her husband that she wouldn't live past Christmas after being diagnosed with eosinophilia, a white blood cell condition.

"That's the first Christmas I ever spent away from my family and children," she said in the Channel Nine interview as she became emotional.

"Nick was four or five. When I came out of hospital George (Giorgos) said that the doctor said 'you won't live past Christmas'. But I was so determined because my kids needed me still. I wanted to give them everything.

"I had a very happy childhood but when I came to Australia it was the worst time of my life. Absolute worst. I was lonely. I didn't want my kids to ever feel like they didn't have someone. Time is what I gave them. A lot of time. I'm happy. I'm good. I don't know why I'm crying all the time. I'm good."

Nill and her son have a close bond now. "I love it," she said. "He's very kind and he's loving. He tells me he loves me every day. He cuddles. He doesn't care if I cuddle him in front of people or give him a kiss. That's the kid that I love. And I always wanted to do that, but he shied away from it for a bit.

"When he was little we were so close. It's nice to have him back. It's really nice. I'm happy for him. He's happy and enjoying life and appreciating every little thing. It's a good feeling."

Kyrgios was asked about his mother after reaching the Wimbledon semi-finals: "Obviously my mum's health has been a bit rocky. I mean, it's been pretty bad for a while now. And obviously, she is not able to kinda come.

"She is not allowed to travel that much. But even in the Australian open, she won't come to my matches because she got like a pacemaker and stuff, too stressful. So yeah, I try to talk to her. She will wake up in the morning and say, 'oh I saw the scores. It looks like you had a tough match,' and I'm just 'like you have no idea,'" he said.

The health of his mother and father was also on his mind when he reached the US and he was keen to get home as soon as he could after the US Open.

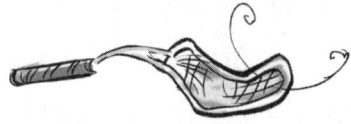

Nick Kyrgios is not the only still active tennis player to succumb to the pressures of elite competition.

The scenes of Andrey Rublev's emotional mid-match breakdown in his US Open quarter-final in September 2022 (a day after the Kyrgios meltdown), were difficult to watch but served to remind fans what players can go through when big matches are in the balance. Yes, it may be only a game but the pressure is enormous.

Commentators and critics often react adversely when athletes – particularly at elite level – display dissent, rage and violent disappointment.

Should athletes always appear as emotionless robots?

All humans have their flaws.

Rublev explained previously how depression had impacted him, just as Kyrgios did when talking about his "darkest periods".

Both had support teams, but their emotions overwhelmed them in the two days of the quarter-finalks when so much was at stake in their career ambitions.

They both have a team around them but head out on court on their own and both struggled to contain their emotions in high-stakes quarter-final defeats in the last two days.

The reaction to Rublev crying and biting down on a tennis ball after conceding a third-set break was not the same as for Kyrgios's racquet-mashing explosion immediately.

But the underlying emotions probably were similar.

Rublev also was well known in tennis for on-court explosions and breaking racquets. But his outlet was much different at Flushing Meadows.

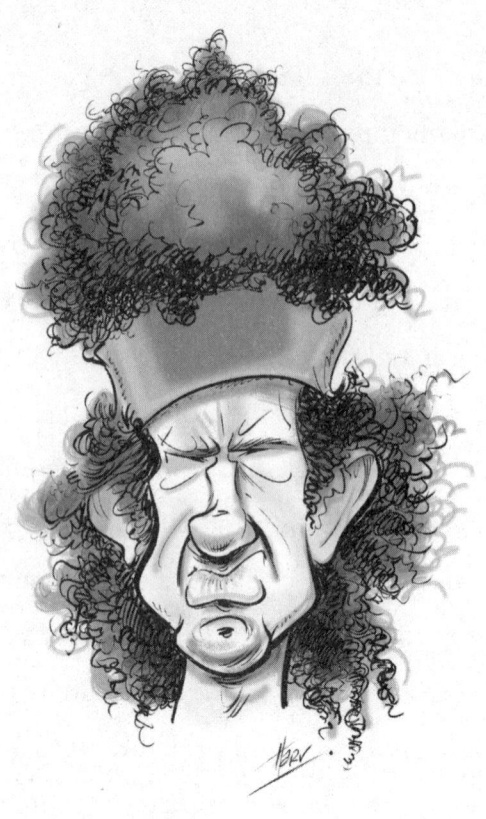

"He's a fantastic talent but you've got to be able to put it together, you've got to be able to compete on a regular basis and unfortunately Nick hasn't been able to do that for a while."

JOHN McENROE

MIND GAMES

There are two ways of looking at how Nick Kyrgios behaves on court; it might reflect what is going on in his own mind, or it might be about getting into the minds of his opponents. Possibly it's both.

Some have at times questioned his mental state. Kyrgios has made no secret about his mental demons and efforts to treat and suppress them.

Just what role those demons play in his actions that divide opinion in the world of professional tennis is up for debate. It's complex.

He's now a Wimbledon finalist but has he laid the demons to rest? Wimbledon saw the best and worst of his on-court behaviour – some brilliant tennis and some temper tantrums.

At his press conference after losing the Wimbledon final, Kyrgios touched on mental aspects of playing top level tennis when asked if he was motivated for a return to have another shot at the championship.

"It takes a hell of an athlete mentally and physically to win one of these things," he said. "I think eight people have won this title since I've been born. It shows physically one thing, obviously it shows. Mentally it's another beast. To come back here for two weeks in a row. None of the people in this room understand it.

"It's just different. Like the social media, the things you have to deal with, like for me it hasn't been easy the last three or four days to block everything out on socials, just everything, and try and just find the balance. It's so easy to access all that stuff. I've really tried to make a conscious effort of trying to focus on the task on hand.

"I don't think past tennis players understand that either, like the older guys. They don't understand how much negativity and opinions get thrown your way. It's hard. It's really hard to deal with all that.

"I commend Federer, Djokovic, and Nadal. These guys, what they deal with must be insane. And that is, for me, that shows the sign of a champion. That's what they deal with, as well, and then being able to perform, it's incredible."

Some commentators have tried to rationalise his approach, but most seem confident that it is what is holding him back from reaching his potential.

Australian Davis Cup captain Lleyton Hewitt, a former winner at Wimbledon, former World No. 1 and winner of 30 tournaments, seems to understand Kyrgios more than most.

He told Kyrgios after he lost to Djokovic that he should be proud of not just making the final but everything he did during the grass court season.

Hewitt, inducted into the International Tennis Hall of Fame in July 2022, said his role as Davis Cup captain limited his options to be with Kyrgios on a more regular basis.

Kyrgios last played Davis Cup tennis in November 2019.

"We'd absolutely love to have him playing for us," Hewitt said.

"We're a much stronger side if he's available and can play for us. And he's an option for singles and doubles matches, which is important in this format.

"To have that kind of weapon at your disposal, we'd certainly want him to be part of that if possible."

(There was no appearance by Kyrgios in Australia's 2022 Davis Cup campaign).

Kyrgios appreciated the support shown by Hewitt, noting that some other Australian tennis legends were instead "tearing me down."

At a press conference before the final, Kyrgios said that of all the champions in Australian tennis, he felt only Davis Cup captain Lleyton Hewitt had been on his side.

"As for the greats of Australian tennis they haven't always been the nicest to me. They haven't always been supportive. They haven't been supportive these last two weeks," he said.

"The kind of only great that has been supportive of me the whole time is Lleyton Hewitt.

"He knows that I kind of do my own thing... he knows to keep his distance and let me do me."

Kyrgios's outbursts against crowds, officials and even his own supporter group leave people wondering about his state of mind, commitment and dedication.

John McEnroe, former World No. 1, once himself a "brat" and much more recently a commentator, knows a bit about the demons that can get in the mind of an elite sportsperson, specifically champion tennis players.

Speaking after Kyrgios lost to Daniil Medvedev in the second round of the Australian Open in January 2022, McEnroe said it was tough to watch Kyrgios not fulfilling his obvious potential.

"I like Nick as a person, I coached him at the Laver Cup four times. He's a good kid," McEnroe told Alize Lim and Mats Wilander in the Eurosport Cube.

"But it's tough to watch because he's so talented, so great for the game. I would love to see him step up and be in the top five or six players, where I think he belongs."

McEnroe has some knowledge of the Kyrgios psyche.

He was asked what stopped Kyrgios from beating Medvedev in the Australian Open early in 2022. "Between his ears, that's what's missing," McEnroe said. "He's got great game. I would say tennis-wise, the most talented player I've seen in the last 10 years."

He said Kyrgios had the talent but not the commitment and dedication required to reach the top.

"Look at Roger Federer, Rafael Nadal and Novak Djokovic (co-incidentally all three had been beaten by Kyrgios early in his career).

"These consummate pros who do whatever it takes to win and they look at Nick, they realise he's great for the game," McEnroe continued. "He's got a personality, he's a smart kid, he's a good kid, everyone likes him.

"He's a fantastic talent but you've got to be able to put it together, you've got to be able to compete on a regular basis and unfortunately Nick hasn't been able to do that for a while."

Six months later and Wimbledon 2022, McEnroe continued to talk about the player Kyrgios still had not become.

"It's unbelievable, he moves the needle for us in tennis. We need this big time but we don't need him to try half the time."

McEnroe said he believed fear of failure was keeping Kyrgios from producing his best tennis all the time.

"He's a good kid, the players like him, he's well liked in the locker room, he does a lot of charity work," he said.

"But he's got demons you know, in a way — we all have this fear of failure and it's a question of how you best deal with it."

If it's a question of confidence, only just a week after the Wimbledon final another Australian showed what confidence can do by winning a golf major in Scotland to become the Champion Golfer of the Year and become No. 2 in the world. Cameron Smith remained bullish through all four rounds of the championship. He could have thrown it all away on the third day after giving up a lead and trailling by four shots.

But that's not the way he is. Even on the last day when he was three behind leader Rory McIlroy, Smith still believed he had a chance. Few others did. It took a comeback for the ages. "I've definitely kicked myself a couple of times over the past few years. To do it the way I did today was pretty cool to be back and really apply pressure, keep holing putts. It was awesome," Smith said.

Yes, tennis is different, but self-belief isn't.

Speaking to Tennis365, John McEnroe suggested he had

sympathy for the battles Kyrgios has had. He spoke about his own battles with mental health issues.

McEnroe's troubles have been chronicled in a movie about his life. He said he hoped Kyrgios embraced the possibilities in front of him.

Of Kyrgios he said: "We are all assessing the odds of whether he will commit to tennis now and while I have doubts that he will, I'd love to see him do it.

"We want to see this guy on a tennis court and would rather not be guessing when he is going to shout at his box. I am probably not one to talk about being angry on court because I had my own problems in that department, but I hope Nick sees what's possible here.

"Forget the stuff where he's screaming and yelling because his shot making is incredible. Okay hitting between your legs on pretty important points is not normal, but this guy pulls it off most of the time.

"Hopefully he'll decide that something is worth making the commitment for a couple of years. I'm not thinking that it's likely, but hopefully I'm wrong. I want to be wrong because Nick going all-in with tennis would be incredibly positive for our sport."

Most criticism is levelled at Kyrgios for specific behavioural incidents, not the quality of his tennis.

His conduct during the men's singles final at Wimbledon in 2022 drew the ire of several former players, compatriots Pat Cash and Renae Stubbs among the most prominent critics.

In a harsh attack, Cash accused Kyrgios of cheating, abuse and dragging tennis down to new depths.

In the BBC commentary box for Kyrgios's match against Tsitsipas, Cash said described that match as "absolute mayhem."

"Is it entertaining? Yeah, possibly," he said. It's gone to the absolute limit now."

Cheating? When pressed on that point, Cash said: "(It's) the gamesmanship, the abuse he was giving.

"Tsitsipas would make a line call and (Kyrgios) would go up there and start complaining, he'd be in his face. That's part of gamesmanship, that's the sort of stuff he does and I think there's a limit.

"I have no problems with a bit of gamesmanship but, when it gets to that level, I think it's just out of control.

"As it was, the umpire lost control. The ball kids were running across the court as Kyrgios was serving. He didn't slow down for any of that stuff.

"Tsitsipas got sucked right into it, so it was entertaining and fascinating but for me I"s gone too far now."

Rennae Stubbs, former player and more recently coach and commentator, didn't hold back when criticising Kyrgios for yelling at his support crew courtside: "Honestly, this behaviour of yelling at your box because they aren't doing what u want, is actually beyond ridiculous," she Tweeted.

"THEY CAN'T READ YOUR MIND! Yes this is his way of dealing with pressure, I get it but this is straight up constant abuse to people that love you, it's embarrassing."

But the quality of his Kyrgios's play drew praise.

Goran Ivanisevic, former player and coach of Kyrgios's Wimbledon conqueror Novak Djokovic, described Nick Kyrgios as a tennis genius, saying it had been difficult to make a game plan for the Wimbledon final.

"He is a genius, a tennis genius. He doesn't know what he's going to play next in the point. We just concentrated on what Novak had to do, the things he had to be careful (with), Ivanisevic said.

"When somebody is serving like Nick Kyrgios, for me the best server in the game by far, an unbelievable tennis player, it is very unpredictable.

"So it's impossible to make tactics. 15 minutes, (against Djokovic) the best returner in the world, he does not touch (Kyrgios's) serve. You need to take every chance you get because you don't have too many chances."

The world may get insight into the world of Nick Kyrgios in the Netflix documentary about world tennis that followed several players who signed up to take part throughout the course of the 2022 tennis season.

Kyrgios and girlfriend Costeen Hatzi co-operated with the makers, giving interviews and being filmed, Kyrgios being the player they chose to follow at Wimbledon.

He said when asked about the documentary: "I think I was quite interested because I think tennis culture is changing. I think there is a lot of, I mean, there is no hiding it. Tennis is a very white privileged sport. I loved the fact that I was able to show my path and the way I go about it and how I connect with people. I think it's a very different side to how people would perceive most tennis players."

McEnroe said that like he (McEnroe) did nowadays, Kyrgios may regret some of his outbursts and how they ultimately may affect his career.

"I would say I'm proud of most of what I did but there are certainly times where I'm like, 'I didn't need to do that'," he said.

"It only exacerbated the situation and made more people get mad at me or start booing me so it wasn't like it helped me.

"It may be at times you blow off some steam. Obviously, you see Kyrgios doing that all the time.

"How do you think his box feels when he's screaming at them? Those are the people that love him most, right?

"Unfortunately, the people that you love most you take it out on, because you feel closest to them. I think we can all relate to that. But if it wasn't so sad it would be funny in a way.

"So that part, hopefully he would look at and go, 'I don't need to do that to my dad or my girlfriend'.

"You know he's sitting there and he's obviously tortured in certain ways. (He's) unbelievably talented, very smart... a hell of a player when he wants to be."

Kyrgios gave some insight into how he mentally handles pressure on the court when talking about his five-set win over American Brandon Nakashima where, as tennis writers noted, he showed model behaviour and a new level of focus.

Battling a nagging shoulder injury, Kyrgios doubled down in the final set after dropping the fourth without really threatening – appearing to throw in the towel was how one commentator put it – to secure a victory that propelled him into the quarter-finals.

He said he used a moment at the end of the fourth set to soak in the Wimbledon atmosphere, privately congratulate himself and instead of melting down, talk himself into a calm state.

"That's probably the first time in my career where I wasn't playing well, regardless of playing centre court Wimbledon, fully packed crowd, (and) I was able to just say, 'Wow, look how far I've come', to myself," he said.

"I was bouncing the ball before I served. I really just smiled to myself. I was like, 'We're here, we're competing at Wimbledon, putting in a good performance mentally'.

"I'm just proud of the way I steadied the ship.

"You know he came firing in the fourth set, his level didn't drop. My five-set record is pretty good. Honestly, that's what I was thinking about.

"I've never lost a five-set match here. I was like, 'I've been here before, I've done it before', and I came through again."

Kyrgios said he also drew on his famous quarter-final victory over Rafael Nadal in 2014 to help collect himself mentally.

"I stepped out here against one of the greatest of all time and beat Nadal, so these are all things I had in the back of my mind," he said.

Kyrgios said after the Australian Open in 2022 where he and Thanasi Kokkinakas won the men's doubles title, his goal as a tennis player was to bring new fans to the sport – "I think I want to continue to grow the game."

As for his critics, he said: "I feel like I've definitely had a rough, you know, some up and downs with the Australian public.

"But to be honest, I look at myself in the mirror every day, and I know that I'm comfortable in my own skin.

"You look at some athletes around the world, Neymar, Russell Westbrook ... they're more than just an athlete.

"I have my own foundation, I help kids.

"I'm a platform ... I'm more than just a tennis player."

He said in an interview with ABC Television: "I want to be remembered as more than just someone who played (tennis).

"I want to be remembered as an icon — someone who just went out there and did it their own way."

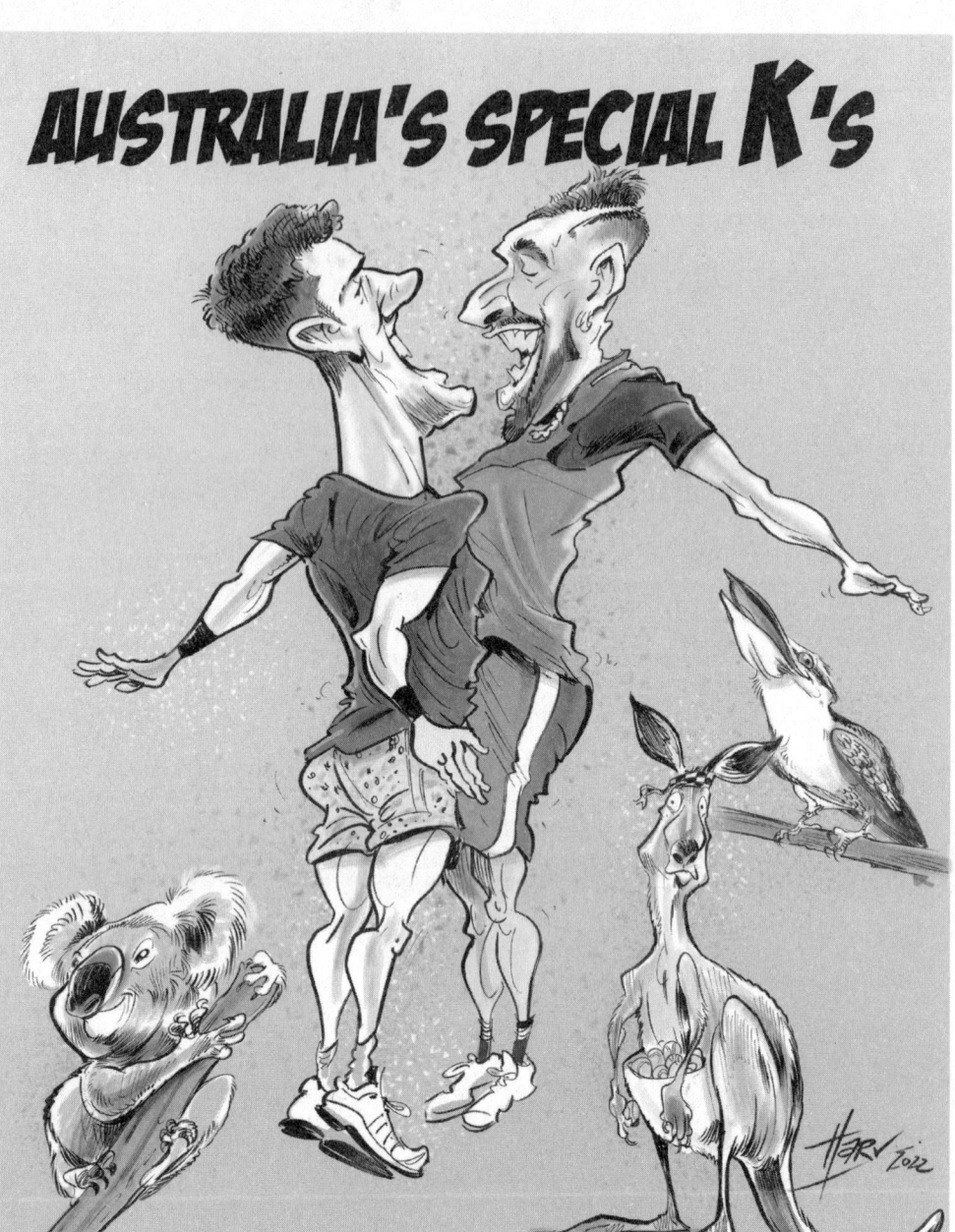

AUSTRALIA'S SPECIAL K's

KOALA, KANGAROO, KOOKABURRA, KOKKINAKIS AND KYRGIOS.

SPECIAL Ks AT THE DOUBLE

Nick Kyrgios still harbours hope of a Grand Slam singles title. In fact, after losing to Djokovic in the Wimbledon final in July 2022 he said he believed he could have won the championship if he had played anyone else.

But could it be that his future in Grand Slam tennis rests elsewhere? Doubles perhaps?

Teaming with friend and fellow Australian Thanasi Kokkinakis he already has a Grand Slam doubles title, the Australian Open in 2022. They went in as wildcard entries.

Kyrgios said afterwards: "For me, honestly you know I thought, I have won some big titles around the world, played some amazing matches. This one ranks number one for me.

"When I say I wouldn't want to do it with anybody else, I mean it. It was just special. The whole week, winning each round, I didn't take it for granted. I was soaking it in.

"Not one time did it cross my mind that we were going to win the title. Maybe when we got to about the quarters I started maybe thinking, but honestly, like the dedication I showed all week for my team, and like, I'm just super proud of myself the way you know, I don't really care too much after I lost to Medvedev but doing it with Kokky is insane."

Kokkinakis added: "To be a Grand Slam champion with my boy, we have known each other since we were eight, nine years old, done some serious things together, have had some serious experiences, but this is incredible. We didn't expect this at all."

Kyrgios and Kokkinakis defeated fellow Australians Matt Ebden and Max Purcell 7-6, 6-4.

A new imposing doubles team was born.

The pair went on to Miami, reaching the semi-finals where they lost to the eventual winners, and reunited successfully again (seeded second) in Atlanta in August 2022 for an ATP 250 title, defeating another Australian pair, Jason Kubler and John Peers 7-6 (4), 7-5.

It was their win at Melbourne that earned them the title, "Special Ks".

They entered the doubles championship at Wimbledon but withdrew as Kyrgios made a charge at the singles crown.

He said after withdrawing from the doubles: "I'm a singles player. My priority has always been singles. I've made quarter-finals here before, I've won singles titles.

"I played nearly four hours in my first round. Me personally, it was just too much time on court.

"Today, I made up for that. But I want to put my singles as my priority. I'm doing what's best for my body."

Kyrgios also was critical of the doubles format in the Open Championship at Wimbledon, the only major with best-of-five sets in men's doubles.

"To be honest, I'm not really looking forward to playing best-of-five sets doubles," Kyrgios said. "I think it's the stupidest thing ever, to be brutally honest.

"I don't know why it's best-of-five sets.

"No one wants to play best-of-five sets doubles, no one wants to watch best-of-five-sets doubles.

"I'm excited, but I'm also dreading the fact that if it's one-set all I'm going to have to be playing three more sets of doubles.

"That's why I haven't played it before, it doesn't make sense because I've always gone pretty well here in singles. I'm not going to, on my off day, play potentially five sets of doubles."

But it is possible Kyrgios started to rethink his singles ambitions and the toll it takes on his body. Doubles, though often a great spectacle, can mean a lighter load on a player, particularly the effort required for serving every second game in singles that isn't helpful when carrying small but niggling injury worries.

Kyrgios changed tack in Atlanta, withdrawing from the singles citing a niggling knee injury, to concentrate on the doubles with Kokkinakis.

Kokkinakis had lost his first-round singles match in straight sets, and Kyrgios said he wanted to give his friend a lift.

"He had a pretty bad loss last week. I think he would be the first to say that," Kyrgios said. "To be able to bounce back and win a doubles title is never easy. Hopefully that's helped him gain a little bit more confidence as well."

The Atlanta win took them to 14-2 playing together for the year. Atlanta has been a happy hunting ground for Kyrgios, the doubles victory following his success there in singles in 2016, when he defeated John Isner.

"Obviously Atlanta is a special place. Won the singles title here and now the doubles. Crowd's amazing and it was a new experience playing two matches in one day as well for a title," Kyrgios said,

"Me and Kokky were pretty resilient and obviously no singles this week, but confidence is at an all-time high in doubles."

Kyrgios and Kokkinakis are close friends off the court and Kokkinakis was happy to be winning titles with him: "Stoked to have won the Atlanta doubles title with Nick. It's always a pleasure playing with him," Kokkinakis said.

"Second title for the year and I think we're getting better. It's been a great week here, a good way to start off the (American) summer in Atlanta ... hopefully we can keep it rolling."

The ATP doubles rankings as of August showed no Top 20 males from singles in the doubles rankings. You just don't see Djokovic, Nadal or Federer playing Grand Slam doubles, any doubles appearances usually confined to team events. It is not the same in women's tennis where top ranked players often compete in tournament doubles, regarding the matches as equal to or better than practice.

Kyrgios was ranked No. 27 in doubles after Atlanta, Kokkinakis at 24. The two went their separate ways after Atlanta, Kyrgios going to Washington for the Citi Open, scene of his best ATP Tour victory back in 2019. Kokkinakis went to Mexico for an ATP 250 tournament where he was seeded seven in the singles.

Kyrgios teamed up again with American Jack Sock in the

doubles in Washington where they claimed the title in straight sets. The "Special Ks" said they would reunite for the US Open doubles.

Sock was on the losing team in Atlanta but had played doubles with Kyrgios previously, winning an ATP 250 tournament in Lyon, France, in 2018.

Thanasi Kokkinakis and Nick Kyrgios started their quest for a third title of the season with a 6-0, 6-4 victory over Italians Simone Bolelli and Fabio Fognini at the Western & Southern Open in Cincinnati.

The Australians fired eight aces and saved the one break-point they faced, winning in an hour.

The first-round win gave the "Special Ks" their fifth success win. They bowed out in the second round, going down to top seeds Rajeev Ram and Joe Salisbury. The second-round appearance gave Kyrgios a career high No. 18 ranking in ATP doubles with a 19-5 win/loss record. Kokkinakis was ranked No. 23.

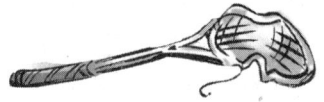

Thanasi Kokkinakis, from Adelaide, is a year younger than Nick Kyrgios. As at 1 August 2022 he was the No. 4 ranked Australian male singles player (behind Alex De Minuar, James Duckworth and Kyrgios), and No. 75 on the ATP world rankings.

His profile on tennis.com: "Began playing tennis when he was eight years old ; Goal to be No.1 in the world and play Davis Cup for Australia; most influential people on his career to date are his brother, parents and his first coach; represented Australian in the ITF World Junior Tennis Competition in 2010; finalist in the Australian Open 2013 boys' singles championships (lost to Nick Kyrgios); won Wimbledon boys 2013 doubles with Nick Kyrgios; first-round victory at Australian Open 2014 (was first tour-level victory; made Davis Cup debut for Australia in February 2014 against France (contested a dead rubber); captured first professional title at ITF Futures event in Saskatoon, Canada; won his first Davis Cup live rubber for Australia in a 2015 World Group first round tie v Czech Republic, coming from two-sets-to-love; underwent shoulder surgery in late 2015; did not play in 2016; returned in 2017 with wins over World No.10 Milos Raonic at Queen's Club and No.15 Tomas Berdych at Los Cabos; teamed with fellow Australian Jordan Thompson to win the 2017 Brisbane International, his first ATP doubles title; sidelined in early 2020 with glandular fever; won Australian Open 2022 men's doubles title and the Atlanta doubles with Nick Kyrgios."

THE KYRGIOS FILE

Nicholas (Nick) Hilmy Kyrgios.

World ranking 12 September 2022 (after US Open): No 20, up from 25 (before US Open). Became Australia's No. 1 male player after US Open, passing Alex De Minaur who dropped to No. 22.

2022 Record: 12 tournaments, one title, two finals. 35-10 win/loss.

Total career prizemoney (singles/doubles at 9 September 2022, after US Open): $US 12,297,060 ($A 18,150,460).

Birth date: 27 April 1995

Born: Canberra (ACT) Australia.

Father: Giorgos ("George") of Greek origin; **mother**, Norlaila ("Nill") of Malay origin. George is a house painter and Nill is a retired computer engineer. He has two siblings – Christos and Halimah.

Birthstone: Diamond.

School: Radford College to 8th grade, senior years at Daramalan College Canberra to 2012.

Started playing tennis: Age 6.

Early teens: Played basketball before switching to tennis aged 14. Was a promising junior basketball player who represented the Australian Capital Territory and Australia.

Scholarships: Australian Institute of Sport, age 16.

Development: Relocated training base to Melbourne Park in 2013. In 2015 returned to Canberra after the Lyneham Tennis Centre undertook a $A 27 million redevelopment. He donated $A 10,000 to the Centre.

Lives: Luxury home in Sydney, Nassau (Bahamas) and formerly Canberra.

Net worth: Websites that track this kind of information put it at $US 15 million – about $US 12 million plus brand partnerships with companies such as Nike and Beats.

Endorsements: Yonex, Nike, Beats (headphone company).

Singles titles: Washington (Citi) Open 2022; Washington Open 2019; Mexican Open 2019; Brisbane International 2018; Japan Open 2016; Atlanta Open 2016; Open 13 Provence 2016.

Doubles titles: Washington (Citi) Open 2022 (with American Jack Sock), Atlanta 2022 (with fellow Australian Thanasi Kokkinakis), Australian Open 2022 (with Thanasi Kokkinakis), Lyon Open (2018 with American Jack Sock).

Big moments: July 2014 defeated world No. 1 Rafael Nadal in the fourth round of the Wimbledon championships, becoming the first teenager to defeat a world No. 1 in a Grand Slam event since 2005 (when Nadal defeated Federer in the French Open); also the first man to do so ranked outside the top 100 since 1992. Played the Wimbledon final against Novak Djokovic 2022 (lost).

Claim to fame: Kyrgios is only the third player, after Slovakian Dominik Hrbatý and fellow Australian Lleyton Hewitt, to have beaten each one of the Big Three (Novak Djokovic, Roger Federer, and Nadal) the first time he played them. Nadal, 2014 Wimbledon; Federer 2015 Madrid; and Djokovic 2017 Acapulco. Defeated World No. 1 Daniil Medvedev twice in a month in 2022, At Montreal and Flushing Meadow.

Favourite surface: Grass – "On grass, you know, I would be top-5, top-10 in the world, definitely. If I'm feeling good on grass, I feel really, really comfortable on it." He has mostly played on hard courts.

Least favourite surface: Clay. When the ATP announced a clay tournament in Switzerland in the lead-up to the US swing including the US Open he asked: "Why is there clay leading up to the US Open swing? (The US Open is a hardcourt event on a surface called Pro DecoTurf, a multi-layer cushioned surface and classified by the International Tennis Federation as medium-fast).

Biggest tournaments won: 2019 and 2022 Citi Open, Washington.

Looking to 2023: Likely to start the year in the world's top 20 and seeded at the Australian Open and hometown favourite.

Strengths: Aggressive baseline player. One of the most potent first serves in the game, can serve up to 145 miles per hour (233 km/h). Powerful forehand and uses an abbreviated backswing on both his serve and forehand. His backhand, however, is considered his weak point. Has a drop-shot that wins many points.

All-time tournament singles record (to 9 September 2022):

Court Type	Win	Loss
Grass Court	36	18
Clay Court	27	22
Hard Court	140	73
Carpet Court	1	1
Indoor Hard Court	10	4
Grand slam matches	54	31

NB: Walkovers not counted as a win in statistics.

JUNIOR TENNIS

First junior match: 2008 at a Grade 4 tournament in Australia. First International Tennis Federation (ITF) junior title: June 2010, Fiji, age 15.

Junior Grand Slam debut: 2011 Australian Open.

Junior progress: 2012 won two junior Grand Slam boys doubles titles (with Andrew Harris at Roland-Garros, France, and Wimbledon, England). Gained junior world No. 3 ranking. Was to contest the Australian Open Men's Wildcard playoff but withdrew because of injury.

In 2013 he took over the No. 1 ranking by defeating Wayne Montgomery in the Traralgon International final. He entered the Australian Junior Open as No. 3 seed, defeating fellow Australian and doubles partner Thanasi Kokkinakis to claim his first – and only – junior Grand Slam singles title. He and Kokkinakis won the boys doubles at Wimbledon that year.

PROFESSIONAL

Turned professional, joined Association of Tennis Professionals (ATP) men's Tour: 2013.

First year as a professional: Started 2013 ranked 838. Played first professional tournament of the year at the 2013 Brisbane International, losing in the first round of qualifying to fellow Australian James Duckworth. He then lost in the first round of qualifying at the 2013 Australian Open to American Bradley Klahn in straight sets.

At the 2013 Nature's Way Sydney Tennis International, he defeated fellow Australian Matt Reid in straight sets in the final to win his first Challenger Tour (young players hoping to graduate to the main ATP Tour) title at the age of 17.

First main draw in a Grand Slam: 2013 French Open. Given a wildcard into the qualifying competition but when fellow Australian John Millman withdrew, he was raised to the main draw of a Grand Slam for the first time. In the first round Kyrgios had the biggest win of his career to then, against former world No. 8 Radek Štěpánek in three sets, each ending in tiebreaks, giving him the first ATP Tour level win of his career. He lost to Marin Čilić in the next round, but his ranking rose to 213.

Qualified for the 2013 US Open, where he was beaten by fourth seed David Ferrer in his opening match. He reached a new career high of No. 186 on 9 September 2013. In October, reached the semi-final of the 2013 Sacramento Challenger, before falling to Tim Smyczek. He ended his first pro year with a singles ranking of 182.

ATP Tour

Playing weight: 85 kg.

Height: 193 cm (6'4").

Plays: Right-handed. Two-handed backhand.

ATP singles titles won: 7, all on hardcourts –Tokyo, Atlanta, and Marseille in 2016, Brisbane in 2018, and Acapulco and Washington in 2019, Washington in 2022. Finals reached – Nine. Wimbledon debut: 2014, reached the quarter-finals by defeating Rafael Nadal, the first male tennis player to reach the last eight in his first year.

Highest singles world ranking: No. 13 on 24 October 2016. He won 3 ATP singles titles that year.

Lowest world ranking: 1618 (entry to rankings) 9 April 2012.

Ranking January 2022 (Australian Open): 122.

Ranking history: Broke into the world Top 100 in July 2017 and stayed there until January 2022; re-entered in April 2022. No. 20 after US Open 2022.

In the ATP Live Race to Turin finals series, Kyrgios's ranking rose 24 places to No. 21 after Washington and to No. 18 after the US Open. The Race to Turin is a calendar-year points race that rewards the top players and eligible Grand Slam champions with a place at the eight-player Nitto ATP Finals play-offs.

NB: Rankings points were not awarded for Wimbledon 2022 after the banning of Russian and Belarus players. If rankings points had been awarded, Kyrgios would have risen to No. 15. Novak Djokovic dropped from No. 3 to No.7 after winning his seventh Wimbledon crown.

First ATP title: 2016 (24 October – Tokyo).

Best Grand Slam results (30 appearances): Reached final at Wimbledon 2022, losing in four sets to Novak Djokovic. Reached three quarter-finals: Wimbledon 2014, Australian Open in 2015, US Open 2022.

BEST WINS BEFORE WIMBLEDON 2022

Stan Wawrinka (4th seed) 2016 Madrid Masters: Kyrgios 7-6 (9/7), 7-6 (7/2). Second round.

David Goffin ATP 500 Japan Open 2017: Kyrgios 4-6, 6-3, 7-5 to win the title, his third for the year.

Novak Djokovic (No. 2, seed 1), Acapulco Mexican Open 2017: Kyrgios 7-6 (11/9), 7-5 quarter-final.

Roger Federer (No. 2, seed 1), Madrid Masters 2015: Kyrgios 6-7 (7/2), 7-6 (7/5), 7-6 (14/12). Round 2, saved two match points).

Rafael Nadal (No. 1) Wimbledon 2014: Kyrgios 7-6 (7/5), 5-7, 7-6 (7/5), 6-3. Fourth round.

DOUBLES

Highlights: Reached second Grand Slam QF as 19-year-old at 2015 Australian Open, becoming youngest quarter-finalist at his home Grand Slam event since 1990.

Won 2022 Australian Open doubles title as 259th-ranked and wildcard entry with fellow Aussie Thanasi Kokkinakis, defeating Ebden/Purcell in the first All-Australian Grand Slam doubles final since the 1980 Australian Open. The pair were dubbed the "Special Ks."

Kyrgios and Kokkinakas withdrew from the doubles at Wimbledon in 2022 for Kyrgios to focus on his tilt at the singles crown.

Won Atlanta doubles (with Thanasi Kokkinakis) and Washington doubles (with Jack Sock) in 2022.

Career-high doubles ranking: No.22 after back-to-back titles in Atlanta and Washington in August 2022.

Doubles record 2022: 9 tournaments, 3 titles, 3 finals, win/loss 21-6.

Career doubles: 63 tournaments. 4 titles, 4 finals. Win/loss 65-54.

AUSTRALIAN TEAMS

Represented: Australia in Davis Cup, ATP Cup and the Olympic Games. He qualified for his first Olympics at Rio 2016 but withdrew through differences with the Australian Olympic Committee. Has played for Team World in the Laver Cup (Team Europe v Team World tournament).

Kyrgios once said that events such as the Davis Cup, ATP Cup and Laver Cup were his favourites because he preferred the mateship and spirit of being part of a team.

But he hasn't always been available or selected for Australian teams. In October 2021 after the Laver Cup, he made himself unavailable for the Davis Cup in 2022. He said at the time he was wrapping up his season then and wanted to return home to be with his unwell mother.

He represented Australian in 11 Davis Cup tournaments for 17 matches (singles and doubles) from 2013 to 2019 for 11 wins, all in singles (he only played in one doubles match for a loss).

Australia last won the Davis Cup in 2003.

Kyrgios represented Australia once in the now defunct Hopman Cup for mixed teams. He won a doubles match with Daria Gavrilova in Perth when Australia defeated Ukraine in the 2016 final.

OFF THE COURT

The Kyrgios person away from centre court can be quite different. In a blog post in 2021, he revealed he had gone vegan, saying bushfires fires in Australia at that time motivated him to go that way.

He wrote in a post on *Athlete's Voice*, "I've been passionate about animal welfare for some time now. I don't eat meat or dairy anymore. That's not for my health, I just don't believe in eating animals.

"I tried a vegan diet a couple of years ago but with all the travel I do, it was hard to stick to it. Since then I've managed to make it work, and I've been vegetarian for quite a while. Seeing the footage of these animals suffering in the fires only reinforces why I've chosen this diet.

"When I see those terrible photos, I can't comprehend eating meat," he wrote.

In January 2022 Kyrgios partnered with prominent plant-based beef substitute company Beyond Meat in a promotional campaign. He posted on social media: "These guys have come up with something pretty special with their meat-free burger patties."

Reports from Wimbledon said Kyrgios had added some seafood to his diet to compensate for the lack of red meat.

According to an ATP profile on the food of the tennis stars, Kyrgios is a big fan of sushi.

The ATP Food Court writers asked—What's your go-to meal the night before a match? Kyrgios: "Sushi is a good one for me; you get some carbohydrates with the rice, and you can monitor what you've had pretty easily. I like sushi because it's kind of like an event: You go with your friends, your girlfriend or your partner, and it comes out on cute little plates, in cute little pieces, soy sauce, couple of giggles here or there. It's romantic, so... sushi."

You're having friends or family around for dinner, what are you cooking for them? "I'm a big fan of stir-fry noodles, they're like my staple diet. I would probably buy some fresh Atlantic salmon and cut it into slices, maybe for some sashimi or chuck it on the grill. I can also make some good salads, so I'd chop up a couple of salads, mix it in, olive oil, lemon, all that type of stuff."

How do you rate your skills in the kitchen? "I'm actually pretty good, I'm pretty good in the kitchen. I'm a hubby, you know what I mean? I can whip up some good meals."

How long before a match would you eat? "If I'm playing in the afternoon or morning, I won't eat before I play, I'll just have a coffee and get out there. I don't eat too much, and on match days I don't eat much at all."

Is there anything you eat on the court during a match? "Yes, I eat a lot of bananas."

OTHER THAN TENNIS

Investments: Founder of sports media company PlayersVoice. Co-host of No Boundaries podcast with Alexander Babanine.

Vehicles: Car collection has included BMW, Mercedes Benz, Range Rover, Dodge Challenger SRT Demon, Nissan r35 GTR, Tesla Model X.F.

Coach: Hasn't had a permanent one.

Social media: Instagram, Twitter. Website: kyrgios.com, nickkyrgios.net (appear to be inactive).

Favourite Music: Lil' Wayne, Fetty Wap, Drake and Rihanna are choices.

Pastimes: Avid gamer – *Call of Duty: Black Ops Cold War* and *Devil May Cry*. *"I personally believe that I'm the best gamer on the tennis tour."* His mother Nill said the reason he reached his first Grand Slam final at Wimbledon is that he began enjoying life more by leaving his hotel room instead of being cooped up playing video games.

Religion: Raised as a Greek Orthodox Christian, regularly spotted wearing a gold chain with a crucifix.

Sporting idols: Roger Federer and basketballers Kevin Garnett and Michael Jordan.

Favourite basketball team: Boston Celtics. UK soccer team: Tottenham Hotspur, Australian Football League team: North Melbourne Kangaroos.

TV shows: *Family Guy.*

Body art: Four tattoos. Feather (freedom, independence);

"inspire others" on the corner of his right hand; inscription GOAT with Lebron James, Kobe Bryant and Jordan 1; "Time is Running Out" right forearm; finger tattoo (right middle) – the number 74, the age of his grandmother when she died in 2014 and a tribute to her.

CHARITY

Kyrgios started the NK Foundation in 2015 to create sporting opportunities, and a safe space, for underprivileged young people.

From the NK Foundation web site: "A couple of years ago I had a vision: to build a facility for disadvantaged and underprivileged kids where they could hang out, be safe and feel like they were part of a family. There'd be tennis courts and basketball courts and a gym and an oval to kick a footy. There'd be things to eat and beds to sleep in.

"When I am in Australia it is my intention to be hands on in my facility, running camps, playing with the youth and getting behind our cause.

"We are currently in the process of scoping out land in Melbourne and looking for organisations and businesses to partner us. This dream is going to become a reality."

Kyrgios also played a role in highlighting the bushfire crisis in Australia in 2021, which led to the Rally for Bushfire Relief, donating more than $A 33,000 himself and the appeal raising around $A 5 million.

In the early days of the 2020 Covid pandemic he offered

to personally deliver food in Canberra to those whose incomes had been devastated. "If ANYONE is not working/not getting an income and runs out of food, or times are just tough... please don't go to sleep with an empty stomach," Kyrgios posted on social media.

FAREWELL TO ROGER

On 16 September 2022, twenty-times Grand Slam winner Roger Federer, 41, announced that he was leaving the men's world tennis tour after the year's Laver Cup team event in London.

Nick Kyrgios was one of the many players and officials to honour him on his retirement.

"No one will ever play the game like you," Kyrgios wrote in a social media post.

In an earlier interview he said: "In my opinion, I believe Roger is the greatest of all time. With his skill set, the way he plays the game, I think it's pure. I actually think talent-wise Nadal and Djokovic aren't even close to Roger, talent-wise – just purely based on talent the way Federer plays, his hands, his serving, his volleys... untouchable.

"Roger's chopped me a couple of times. Roger makes you feel like you're really bad at tennis sometimes. He walks around, he flicks his head, and I'm, like, I don't even know what I'm doing out here. Roger is the greatest, for me."

Federer was ranked world No. 1 for 310 weeks, including a record 237 consecutive weeks, and finished as the year-end No. 1 five times. He won 103 ATP singles titles, including 20 Grand Slam singles titles, and a record eight men's singles Wimbledon titles. Between 2003 and 2009 he reached 21 out of the 28 major singles finals played.

VIVE LA DIFFERENCE

Australia's two most prominent players on world tennis tours over the past decade have been Ash Barty and Nick Kyrgios.

Prominence doesn't necessarily equate to success in the case of Kyrgios of course, but he has a profile in tennis above that of many other even better players.

Barty on the one hand was a "team" person, Kyrgios was and remains a showman. That's not to say he is without team support; he has referred to that a number of times, even amid controversy.

The two have been miles apart in their tennis career achievements – Barty won three Grand Slam events before surprising everyone by retiring at 25 years old in March 2022; Kyrgios reached one grand Slam final (which he lost), but at 27 years old in 2022, he may not be finished yet, although he has hinted at retirement a number of times.

The differences extend to how they live their lives, how they prepared for big matches and how they conducted themselves on and off the tennis court. The structure of their support teams could not be more dissimilar.

Barty hardly ever referred to "I" in discussing her tennis. It was always "we" and "team." She often referred to "Team Barty." She oozed humility.

These qualities endeared her to the Australian – indeed world – tennis public. Her coach Craig Tyzer was captain of her team, an unsung hero as many commentators put it.

Australian Billie Jean Cup captain Alicia Molik believes Tyzer cannot be overlooked when talking about Barty's success.

"Such a huge amount of credit needs to be given to 'Tyz' because it can be delicate with a world No. 1," Molik said.

"You can just say, 'Right, let's just keep things the same'. Well, no, they as a team, the two of them, work so well that they keep getting better. It's unbelievable, it's mind-blowing.

"She's very wise, she's such an astute tennis player and person that when she's on court she knows what she's working on and why.

"It's not a matter of hitting balls for no reason. There's always purpose and reason behind what she's doing both for her and for Tyz as well.

"He's been amazing because he's found such a complete player, but he's found so many ways for Ash to get better.

"He's really an unsung hero."

After winning the first of her three Slams, the French Open, Barty said: "For me it was the perfect match. I have an extraordinary group of genuine, authentic people around me. This (win) is just a by-product of all the work that we have done."

Her team included mindset coach Ben Crowe, who also worked with many Australian athletes, including Richmond Football Club (AFL) players and surfer Stephanie Gilmore.

After her Wimbledon victory in 2021, Barty said: "I was just extremely lucky that I was able to have the opportunity to learn how to play the game of tennis but I think being a good human being is absolutely my priority every single day."

The contrasts between Barty and Kyrgios are obvious.

Nick Kyrgios does not even have a coach.

He has been asked often about coaches throughout his career but says they're just not for him.

He told TennisNet: "I just don't think a coach is ready for me and I want to spare him that because it would otherwise be a nightmare. At the current stage of my career, it is already too advanced for a coach because my paths have already solidified. And I just don't like to listen to advice, to be completely honest."

In 2022 he added: "I don't have a coach, I haven't had a coach for four, five years now. I feel like tactically I'm one of the best players on tour, I feel like I'm very tactically switched on."

No coach, but he does have a team, and a tolerant one it must be at that because those in his box at Wimbledon in 2022 got the full force of his frustration in the final against Novak Djokovic.

Who was in his box? His father Giorgos, sister Halimah, manager Daniel Horsfall, physiotherapist Will Maher and girlfriend Costeen Hatzi. Mother Nill and brother Christos stayed at home. He has said he has a hit of tennis with Costeen once or twice a week sometimes.

His explanation of his team: "I just look at my box, look at my team, and know that I've just got the crowd in the palm of my hand and just go out there and ride the wave."

It is not recorded how Kyrgios's team reacted when he launched a tirade at the box during his final with Djokovic.

The first outburst came in the fourth game of the second set when he dropped serve for the first time. He began looking to his box to question why he was having to ask them to support him.

Later in the set, when he had a chance to break back at 0-40 but was unable to convert, Kyrgios reached boiling point.

He began shouting at his team after every point as Djokovic levelled the match. "Say something!" he roared. "It's 0-40. God damn! It's 0-40!"

He blew up again in the ninth game of the third set over his perceived failure of their support: "Why do you stop? 40-0, 40-15 and you just relax! Why?"

Commentators were not impressed. Controversial broadcaster Piers Morgan tweeted: "Kyrgios is such a monumental a**hole. Imagine hurling constant foul-mouthed abuse in a Wimbledon final at your own support team/family for YOUR bad shots?"

Will Maher is probably the key player in the Kyrgios team. Kyrgios told athletesvoice.com in 2018: "Will is my physio and he's brilliant... I will always be grateful for the work he's done to get me out on the court tournament after tournament."

In that 2018 article for athletesvoice.com, Kyrgios listed his team as: Matt Reid, occasional training partner; Norlaila Kyrgios (mother); Christos Kyrgios (brother); John Morris (then agent and manager) Gorgios Kyrgios (father); Carlos Fleming (Morris's business partner) and Will Maher (physiotherapist).

A similarity between the two Australians is their closeness to family. Although Kyrgios has had a strained relationship with family at times, he remained close to his mother and her Malaysian heritage: "It's going to be exciting going back to my mum's roots. I've been to Malaysia a couple of times to see relatives ... I don't know much about mum's history. But hopefully they embrace me over there, too."

He was going back to Australia straight after the US Open in 2022 to see his mother and father, both of whom had health problems.

When Ash Barty stepped away from tennis for a year, one of the reasons was absence from family.

In a 2021 interview after winning a tournament, Ash Barty said: "The best part of my life is without a doubt my family and my team.

"I wouldn't be half the person I am without them, I wouldn't have anywhere near the enjoyment if I couldn't do it with them.

"Being able to share all these cool moments with my professional family, but also my personal family, without them I am nothing."

Barty left tennis on top of the world. Kyrgios hinted in 2022 that retirement might be a couple of years away. Was he serious? Time would tell.

When Barty found the stresses of the tour too much, she stepped away for a year to do something completely different (playing cricket), eventually coming back to tennis better than ever and rising to World No. 1.

It was a different story for Kyrgios who battled through his "dark times" and Covid lockdowns that saw his world rankings slide sharply. He fought on through his mental and physical issues and in 2022 regained some of his best form. But he also felt the pressure of being away from home.

He has spoken of that a number of times: "I was away from home for five and a half months. I don't ever want to do that again." And "just being away from home was the toughest bit. Battling injuries, going to tournaments, and not even playing was tough, but they're not really big problems."

Author Ron Reed noted about the Barty-Kyrgios differences in *Barty, Much More than Tennis* (Wilkinson Publishing): "The other comparison that has often been made, and continues to be, is with her (Barty's) contemporary on the men's side of the game, Nick Kyrgios.

"The enigmatic Kyrgios, who is exactly a year minus three days older than Barty, probably was gifted with even more talent, certainly more flamboyance and flair, but has achieved far less, while his volatile and sometimes offensive behaviour has been the polar opposite.

"While Barty has made the most of her gifts, Kyrgios has largely squandered his, much to the frustration – annoyance, even – of the sporting public, who see it almost as a dereliction of his national duty."

The two had a distinctly different approach to national duty. While Kyrgios had represented Australia in the Hopman Cup, a mixed teams event (since discontinued), he withdrew from

Olympic selection. Barty embraced the Olympics.

At the time, having just withdrawn from his third-round match at Wimbledon with a stomach injury, Kyrgios said playing in Tokyo in 2021 (actually the 2020 Olympics postponed amid the Covid pandemic) without spectators didn't "feel right" with him. The showman.

Barty treasured her silver medal in the doubles, though falling short in the singles. She said: "I'm so excited to be a part of my first Olympic team and the Aussie team. We're 480-strong and to be a part of that for the first time in what will be the most unique Olympic Games ever will be awesome." The team person.

Kyrgios travels to the beat of his own drum. He does not follow the path set down by other great Australian tennis players or indeed those from anywhere else at all.

As the French could say, "vive la difference."

FastScripts Transcripts by ASAP Sports. Other sources: ATP Tour, BBC.com and various media reports as identified.